AUSTRALIAN
SHEPHERD

SMART OWNER'S GUIDE®

By Christina Cox-Evick

FROM THE EDITORS OF
DOGFANCY MAGAZINE

Australian Shepherd, a Smart Owner's Guide®
part of the Kennel Club Books® Interactive Series®
ISBN: 978-1-593787-83-7 ©2011

Kennel Club Books, 40 Broad St., Freehold, NJ 07728. Printed in China.

photographers include Isabelle Francais/BowTie, Inc.; Tara Darling/BowTie, Inc.; Gina Cioli and Pamela Hunnicutt/BowTie, Inc.; Shutterstock.com

For CIP information, see page 176.

If you have brought an Australian Shepherd home from a responsible breeder or a rescue group—or are planning to do so—congratulations! You have fallen in love with one of the most intelligent and versatile of all dogs. The Aussie is truly a can-do canine. Give him a job and an outlet for his energy, and you will have a beautiful, devoted companion for many years to come.

Despite his name, the modern Aussie is considered an American creation. Theories abound concerning his origins, but his ancestors probably came from the Basque region of the Pyrenees Mountains between Spain and France. It is believed that these dogs traveled with Basque shepherds who came to America from Australia in the 1800s, hence the Australian Shepherd moniker.

The Aussie became a fixture around rodeos and horse shows. Awareness of the breed increased sharply with the popularity of Western-style horseback riding following World War II. The Australian Shepherd's incredible trainability makes him a welcome partner on farms and ranches.

Away from the farm, the Aussie has proven his worth as a guide dog for the blind, as a service and therapy dog, and in drug detection and search and rescue work. He is also unrivaled as a performance dog. Whether your interest lies in obedience, agility, or rally, your Aussie's fundamental desire will be to please you. No dog trains himself, but the Aussie's intelligence, enthusiasm, and enviable work ethic will make training your dog a pleasurable experience.

At home, Aussies are a joy and especially fond of children. In many families, the Aussie has been the one-and-only breed for generations. It is not uncommon at breed club events to see Grandma and Mom showing dogs in conformation and competing in agility and rally, and then having the same dogs taken into Junior Showmanship by the younger members of the family.

At home on the range and in front of the hearth, the Australian Shepherd is a do-it-all working dog and companion.

Standing 20 to 23 inches at the shoulder for males and 18 to 21 inches for females, Aussies are sturdy yet compact enough to make great pets in suburbia, as long as their owners find ways to channel all of that energy. The American Kennel Club breed standard calls for a dog that is "solid and muscular without cloddiness." The breed is all about moderation in size, bone, and coat. Aussies should be neither fine-boned and slight nor tall and musclebound.

The Aussie's coat is of medium texture and length, straight to wavy, and weather resistant. Other than thorough brushing a few times a week to remove dead coat and reduce shedding, plus the routine care (nails, ears, teeth) that every dog requires, the Aussie is fairly low-maintenance in the grooming department.

Color is very dramatic in the breed. You will see black, red, and blue or red merle (a marbled pattern), all with or without white markings and/or copper points. Eyes can be brown, blue, amber, or any combination thereof, and the eyes can have flecks and marbling. Many people first fall in love with a shimmery blue merle complete with blue eyes and then learn to appreciate the beauty of the other colors and combinations.

This breed requires exercise; this is something that cannot be said too often. Jog, cycle, play Frisbee in the park, or join an agility or rally club with your Aussie. Leisurely strolls or time alone in the backyard will not be enough for this highly intelligent herding breed. You must wear him out. A tired Aussie is a happy Aussie (and owner!).

In the section on temperament, the AKC breed standard describes the Aussie as

"intelligent, active…with an even disposi- tion; he is good-natured, seldom quarrel- some." What an endorsement!

Allan Reznik
Editor-at-Large, DOG FANCY

Beautiful, intelligent, and adept at countless activities, the versatile Australian Shepherd seems the perfect dog, whether for the single person, married couple, or busy family. Yet a closer look will reveal that the very traits that make the Aussie so versatile make him perfect only when paired with the right home.

When that right home does find him, the Aussie becomes the best all-around dog anyone could hope for. He enjoys spending a day at the lake with the kids, jogging alongside an athletic owner, or competing at an agility trial. An Aussie can do just about anything a person wants him to do—the question usually comes down to whether the owner can keep up! And after a busy day, the Aussie happily joins his owner in some down time.

Is the Australian Shepherd the ideal breed for your home? The answer requires you to research the breed and to evaluate your lifestyle honestly. The extra work you do to assure a good match before you bring an Aussie home can save considerable stress and heartache later. With this in mind, let's take a closer look at the Aussie's personality and needs and the type of home and owner that fit best with the breed.

AN ACTIVE HOME

The energetic Aussie needs ample exercise to prevent him from becoming restless, bored, and potentially troublesome. As a herding dog bred to spend his days running to and fro, controlling and moving herds of sheep or cattle, the Australian Shepherd needs much more than twice-daily walks around the block. He must burn off physical energy with frequent runs, games of fetch, canine sports, or other activities.

The Aussie is also a thinking breed, bred for the ability to solve problems on his own when necessary. Besides physical exercise, he needs mental exercise via daily chores such as fetching the paper or finding lost keys, or through some kind of organized training such as obedience, agility, or rally. If you don't provide suitable activity to keep that clever canine mind engaged, the Aussie will find his own entertainment, and it won't always be to your liking!

Other activities that the Aussie enjoys doing with his owner include walking, jogging or running, hiking, swimming, fetching, and other active pastimes. For people interested in a serious pursuit that ultimately helps others, the Aussie's medium size and strong work instinct make him a good candidate for search and rescue work; this training requires dedication and effort on the part of the owner, too.

LET ME IN

The Aussie loves being near his owner as much as possible and thrives only when living indoors. Relegating an Australian Shepherd to a fenced-in backyard or outdoor kennel leaves the isolated dog looking for ways to occupy himself or trying to find someone to play with. This usually results in digging, barking, escaping, or other problem behaviors.

What about the Aussie's history as an outdoor farm or ranch dog? Stock dogs constantly work under their owners' guidance while moving and controlling their herds, which explains the incredibly strong bonds they form with their owners. Few dogs today live this lifestyle, though, and therefore the Aussie must enjoy time with his owners in other ways, such as overseeing household chores, hanging out with the kids, participating in training or competition, or sharing other family pastimes.

Adding a second Aussie may seem like a good idea for providing the current dog with companionship so that he'll stop engaging in problem yard behaviors, but the dogs may not get along or they may simply enjoy digging, barking, or escaping together. No matter how many Aussies live in a household, they consistently need their owners' attention and companionship to direct their energy and intelligence into acceptable outlets.

ME AND MY SHADOW

In typical herding-breed fashion, the Aussie likes to follow his owner throughout the day so he can keep a protective eye on his favorite person and satisfy his curious mind as to what's going on around the home and yard. Many an Aussie will even follow his owner into the bathroom, apparently fearing that his beloved master will sneak out an unseen door or fall victim to some vicious water monster.

This desire to follow also applies every time the Aussie's owner leaves the house. The dog wants to go along on every family adventure, no matter how mundane.

Don't acquire an active breed like the Australian Sheperd with the idea that taking the dog for walks, going outdoors to play, and doing other activities together will increase your own activity level. Sometimes that works, but other times the dog ends up being rehomed if the owner can't stick to his or her end of the deal. All dogs enjoy some activity, so get one that suits your current lifestyle.

And during those times when he must be left behind, few breeds can look more hangdog than a disappointed Aussie.

Overall, the busy, involved Aussie might drive owners who don't like a dog at their heels a bit crazy. Such folks might prefer a less demanding, more laid-back breed that will contentedly sleep on the couch or lie in the sun as the owners go about their daily routines. But for people who want a dog that is keenly interested in his owners' everyday lives, the Aussie fits perfectly.

FAIR BUT FIRM

As much as he adores his owner, the Aussie will occasionally test his limits, just as children or teenagers push their boundaries to see what they can get away with. Bred to possess the forcefulness to handle troublesome sheep and cattle, the Aussie's natural assertiveness prompts him to check his owner's resolve to be in charge by ignoring commands, barking to demand food, and displaying other pushy behaviors.

As with the unruly youngster who usually gets his way, the Aussie whose owner gives in to the dog's undesirable behavior may end up running the household. Both the dog and you will be happier when you set forth and enforce doggy rules, such as expecting the dog to sit quietly as you prepare his dinner. This kind of structure within his home allows the Aussie to both love and respect the human members of his family.

Of course, a dog with the kind of attitude and brainpower for which the Aussie is known must learn basic obedience—*sit, down, come,* and *stay*, at the very least. This training helps teach the dog self-control and compliance while strengthening the dog/owner bond and producing a mannerly companion who will be welcome at friends' homes, parks, and other locations.

HOME BASE

The Australian Shepherd needs room to run, making a home with a large fenced yard or acreage the ideal setting for him to stretch his legs, sniff about, and enjoy being a dog. That said, unlike dogs who view fences as impenetrable barriers, the thinking Aussie, left outside on his own for too long, starts to see the fence as an inconvenient obstacle to what's beyond and soon figures out how to climb over, jump over, or dig under it.

What this means is that a large fenced yard proves ideal as long as the Aussie's owner joins him or watches him closely during outdoor time. Given a good run several times a day and constructive outlets for his clever mind, the Aussie needn't stay outside by himself, as he will happily follow you about the house as you clean, cook, or perform other indoor tasks.

Though many places sell outdoor kennels made of 6-foot-high chain link or welded wire-mesh fencing in various sizes, these smallish areas work only for intermittent confinement, such as those times when you want your Aussie to enjoy fresh air but stay

Aussies thrive in households that include them in activities as part of the family. They want to be where you are and involved in whatever you are doing, not relegated to the backyard by themselves or in a crate all day long. Be prepared to make a commitment of time and energy as an Aussie owner.

—Jenn Merritt, certified professional dog trainer and Australian Shepherd owner from Efland, North Carolina

To help you decide if you and the Aussie are meant for each other, go places where you can watch the breed in action, like agility trials or herding trials, and also visit several breeders' homes to see what the dogs act like in their everyday setting. This up-close-and-personal view offers insights not available any other way.

safely out of the way when you're doing something such as mowing the lawn. A dog who is kenneled too frequently develops behavior problems, such as barking, pacing, or constant circling, due to boredom.

Like any dog, the Aussie can adapt to various living situations if his exercise requirements are met by a dedicated owner. For instance, he will burn off more energy running 5 miles or swimming away the afternoon with an athletic owner than if left to his own devices in a large fenced yard, so a big yard is not necessary if you are committed to exercising your Aussie in other ways. However, the breed's need for exercise does not decrease during rainy or winter conditions; this is not the breed for fair-weather owners!

Longtime Australian Shepherd owner Jenn Merritt, a certified professional dog trainer through the Association of Pet Dog Trainers, summarizes, "The ideal Aussie owner has an active lifestyle, time to devote to training, especially during the first two years of the dog's life, and the ability to meet the dog's daily physical exercise needs with access to a fenced-in space [in which] to run as well as to provide mental stimulation using toys and games."

An excellent watchdog, the Aussie considers himself guardian of his home, hearth, yard, and vehicle and can get himself into trouble if someone he doesn't know unthinkingly walks into his yard or opens the car door while he's inside. If taught from an early age to accept the comings and goings of kids and teenagers, the Aussie learns to control this instinct, but adult strangers should not enter his territory without your nod.

Within the home, the Aussie raised with children becomes accustomed to the high-pitched voices, quick movements, and other traits that dogs who are unfamiliar with kids can find bewildering and even annoying. This underscores the importance of finding an Aussie with an affinity for children when adopting an older puppy or adult.

Help assure a good relationship between your kids and your new Aussie by teaching children how to act with a puppy or dog before bringing one home. Use a stuffed toy to show youngsters how to gently pet and handle a puppy. If a friend has a child-loving, tolerant adult dog, allow your children to practice what they've learned with your guidance. For safety's sake, after your Aussie comes home, always supervise small children and your dog to make sure that all parties mind their manners.

On another note, every Australian Shepherd home should be equipped with a quality vacuum cleaner unless those who live there don't mind living with fur bunnies blowing about the house. Aussies shed, and when seasonal shedding times kick in, they shed a lot. A thorough twice-weekly grooming usually suffices, but daily brushing is required when the Aussie blows his coat (sheds his undercoat) in preparation for the summer heat.

An active Aussie is a happy Aussie! This athletic breed has energy to spare.

A LITTLE ATTITUDE

The Aussie's success in so many activities rates him as one of the dog world's smartest, most trainable breeds, but this doesn't mean that he slavishly obeys your every whim, even once trained. Part of the Aussie's charm comes from his inquisitive mind. If you tell him to lie down, he may think, "What if I do it this way instead?" and first do a *sit* or bounce between positions.

Such behavior comes not from disobedience but from the breed's strong desire to please coupled with his curiosity and drive to work. With an owner he loves and respects, he will try different responses to see which one makes you happiest. Mixing things up also helps him alleviate boredom. Either way, training is best accomplished with a sense of humor and gentle insistence that your Aussie do things your way.

Despite his "I-can-do-it-better" attitude, the Australian Shepherd will take whatever task you put before him very seriously. If you train him to find your lost keys, he will search intently until he locates them. If you compete in agility, he'll react to your directions at lightning-fast speed and expect you to keep up the pace. This "get-it-done" approach to life endears him to many but can be too much for others to handle.

As mentioned, the Aussie's zest for whatever task his owner asks of him, coupled with superior intelligence and a manageable size, makes him a great prospect for serious jobs, such as search and rescue work. And despite his serious mindset, make no mistake, the Australian Shepherd has a softer, sillier side that he usually reveals only to those he loves. His sense of humor may be displayed through a range of vocalizations, such as sharp barks, yips, or whines, or a sudden thump as he hits the ground and rolls on his back in hopes of a good tummy rub.

In addition to being surprised by the Aussie's lighthearted side, even the most experienced owners can be amazed by the breed's intellect. Longtime fancier Cec Connair of Baltimore, Ohio, discovered the following with one of her Aussies: "This dog has always watched dog shows on television and loves it when the dogs pose and gait around the ring. It's like she's saying, 'I know how to do that!' She recognizes what those dogs are doing, and it's just too funny."

Affectionate with those he loves and sociable with known friends, the Australian Shepherd typically meets new people with reserve rather than with tail-wagging, face-licking greetings. The breed's inherently reserved nature makes frequent and ongoing socialization starting in puppyhood very important. As your Aussie encounters a variety of people, other dogs, and life experiences in general, he learns that the world and those who live in it are quite pleasant.

Did You Know?

In a ten-year span from 1999 to 2009, the Australian Shepherd rose from thirty-eighth in popularity among American Kennel Club-registered breeds to twenty-eighth, a rise unfortunately accompanied by a corresponding increase in the number of Aussies turned over by their owners to breed rescues and shelters.

The herding instinct remains strong in the Aussie and sometimes results in his nipping people's heels, particularly those of "his" children, as he attempts to herd them like he would his flock. The Aussie likes his family where he can keep an eye on everyone. Because his well-intentioned nips hurt, though, an owner must direct this tendency from day one into suitable outlets, guiding the Aussie into games of fetch, playing with toys, and chewing safe bones to prevent a bad habit from ever forming.

Chasing moving objects is another instinct related to the Australian Shepherd's herding heritage, and this must be directed properly in today's crowded society. Chasing bicyclists, joggers, cars, or other passersby can be dangerous for all concerned. Start teaching your dog what he can and can't chase as soon as he comes home with you—joggers and cars, no; balls and Frisbees, yes. Again, by never allowing inappropriate behavior in the first place, you forestall a problem.

OTHER PETS

Though the Aussie does fine as an only dog when he receives the daily interaction and exercise he needs, most dogs enjoy canine companions with whom they can run, play, and explore the yard when their owners' attention turns elsewhere. Pairing dogs usually works best when combining sexually altered dogs of opposite sexes, which both negates the possibility of unwanted puppies and increases the likelihood that they'll get along.

Keep in mind that another dog will never be a substitute for your attention. With two Australian Shepherds, you increase the devotion and love you get twofold, but you also increase the amount of training,

The Australian Shepherd should not be a hyper dog; he should be able to go out and work hard for half the day but then settle under the truck for the afternoon while his owner fixes the fence. That's how the Aussie of old has been, and I think that's the ideal temperament for the breed.

—Terry Martin, longtime breeder and ranch-dog owner from Hico, Texas

exercise, and time required by you to give the dogs the individual attention that they crave. For owners who enjoy these facets of Aussie ownership, having two dogs doubles the fun; for those who do not, it simply doubles the work.

Anyone considering two Aussies should also consider what happens if the two dogs do not get along. Even a male/female combination does not always work out. A professional trainer can sometimes resolve the dogs' issues, but not every owner can keep the peace once the trainer leaves. In this event, would you keep the two dogs separated or find one of them a good home? Chances are, this situation won't arise, but be aware that it can.

Many Australian Shepherds coexist peacefully or even companionably with cats, particularly when introduced to them at a young age. Some Aussies, usually those raised with small animals such as rabbits, hamsters, or guinea pigs, live amenably with these pets, but this combination can be risky because Aussies tend toward a strong prey drive, meaning the instinct to chase and grab small game (or what they perceive as game).

Obviously, this prey and chase instinct carries over to livestock kept as pets, so folks who have horses, goats, or other large animals that they do not want to be herded will have to teach their Aussies that those animals are off limits. As usual, this will be more easily accomplished when starting with a puppy or very young dog that can be taught before bad habits start. Stopping an Aussie from engaging in this natural behavior once established proves considerably more difficult.

I NEED YOU

At times, the Aussie seems a contradiction— a tough, independent-thinking herding dog on one hand, but a sensitive, completely devoted companion on the other. Yet these seemingly opposing forces are what make this breed the supreme working dog that he is, as he stoically withstands the rigors and hardships of working with animals many times his size while at the same time willingly and instantly responding to his master's directions.

This combination can puzzle novice owners, especially those who try to train the Aussie based on his rugged image rather than considering his total character. Treat the Australian Shepherd harshly, and you lose his adoration; treat him indulgently, and you lose his respect. Instead, be consistent, show him what is wanted, and gently insist that he always comply, and then you'll discover the trainability that this breed is famous for.

Another part of developing the Aussie's trainability and character involves socialization. A puppy kindergarten class exposes the puppy to new people, other puppies, a new environment, and so on, but socialization cannot stop there with this naturally reserved and sometimes wary breed. In

Did You Know? Despite those picturesque movie scenes of sheep grazing on the hillsides with shepherd dogs quietly watching over them, in real life, sheep and especially cattle will physically challenge the dogs' authority, hence the need for the assertive, tough Aussie that can convince uncooperative stock to do as he bids.

fact, all dogs, regardless of breed or mix, need ongoing and consistent exposure to various locations, people of all ages and races, other dogs, and life experiences.

The good news is that the Aussie loves nothing better than accompanying his owner wherever possible. As a puppy, your Aussie should be taken for very short car rides initially and gradually worked up to longer rides. Though a young pup must be crated for safety, once he matures a bit and becomes comfortable in the car, he can be safely strapped in with a car harness if desired so he can enjoy the view.

The Australian Shepherd is prized for his work ethic, companion qualities, and stunning good looks.

Whether running errands, going to the lake for a day of swimming, joining the family for a cookout, or embarking on a longer road trip, the well-socialized Aussie with good basic obedience training makes a wonderful companion. In addition, he doesn't backseat-drive, talk your ear off, or sing off-key to the radio…what more could anyone ask of a travel buddy?

All in all, the Australian Shepherd is an intelligent, devoted, and ready-for-anything companion suitable for a smart, active, and dedicated owner who wants a dog to share in his or her life. If you're among those who appreciate and understand this breed's many facets and realize that you and the Aussie are truly a match made in heaven, then you will find your Aussie happily following you to the ends of the earth.

Show your artistic side. Share photos, videos, and artwork of your favorite breed at Club Aussie. You can also submit jokes, riddles, and even poetry about Aussies. Browse through our various galleries and see the talent of fellow Aussie owners. Go to **DogChannel. com/Club-Aussie** and click on "Galleries" to get started.

JOIN OUR ONLINE **Club Aussie**™

The Thinker

Dog trainers like Cec Connair of Baltimore, Ohio, know that true canine intelligence goes beyond the aptitude to learn obedience or manners—it relates to the individual dog's ability to solve problems without anyone's help, an area in which the Aussie shines. But when her young Australian Shepherd caught her long line on a railroad tie along the driveway, what happened next surprised even Connair.

"Years ago, I was using a 50-foot long line on a four-month-old puppy to train her to some outside boundaries and to come when called. We were working in the front yard along the driveway when I decided to wrap things up and go inside the house. When I called Breena, she immediately started to come to me but then got her line, which I had put a few knots in, caught on one of the railroad ties lining the driveway," says Connair.

Though ready to go to her aid if needed, Connair decided to wait and offer Breena some motivation. She says, "I talked to her in an encouraging tone, telling her, 'C'mon, you can figure this out.' For a short time, Breena stood there and looked at me, puzzled about what she should do." Connair kept encouraging Breena, knowing that the pup had the genetics to solve her dilemma. "Her mom was extremely bright," says Connair.

Next thing she knew, "This very young puppy turned, walked to the very spot where the long line was caught, picked it up in her teeth, pulled it loose, and came happily running over to me," says Connair, who was stunned at the adept manner in which this baby Aussie had freed herself. "That was an incredibly clever move for any dog, but especially for such a young puppy," she says.

Fortunately, Connair directed this puppy's intelligence and problem-solving ability toward obedience and other types of training; otherwise, who knows what trouble such a bright Aussie might have gotten herself into? Though Aussie breeder Connair says that those sharp minds still surprise her every day, none have outdone that young puppy's reasoning.

An Aussie trains on the pause table. In a true test of discipline, each dog in agility competition must break the fast pace of the course and stop on the table for a specified amount of time.

THE AUSSIE OUTLINE

This herding dog has it all!

COUNTRY OF ORIGIN: United States

WHAT HIS FRIENDS CALL HIM: Aussie

SIZE: Males: 21 to 23 inches; females:18 to 21 inches

OVERALL APPEARANCE: Balanced, medium in size, muscular, and lithe; tail is naturally bobbed or docked

COAT: Medium-length double coat that is shorter on the head, ears, front of forelegs, and below the hocks, with feathering on the back of forelegs and between the tail and hocks

COLOR: Blue or red merle (base color marbled with white), black, or red, all with or without white and/or tan markings

PERSONALITY TRAITS: Smart, trainable, energetic, affectionate with family, aloof with strangers

WITH KIDS: Good with kids when raised with them

WITH OTHER ANIMALS: Generally fine with dogs of the opposite sex, but can be jealous about sharing owner's attention; usually respects cats when raised with them but is risky around small pets such as hamsters and guinea pigs

ENERGY LEVEL: High; needs physical and mental activity daily

GROOMING NEEDS: Twice-weekly brushing, bathing as needed; daily brushing during shedding

TRAINABILITY: All training must be done with motivational methods that engage the dog's active mind

LIVING ENVIRONMENT: Adaptable but best in a home with a large fenced yard

LIFESPAN: Average 11 to 13 years

istory proves infinitely more interesting when steeped with mystery, and in that regard, the history behind the Australian Shepherd does not disappoint. Breed fanciers debate the exact origin and blending of breeds that created the versatile dog we know today. We do know that the stockmen who developed the Aussie sought only to produce a supreme working dog, with the breed's good looks occurring as a fortunate happenstance.

Many people find it surprising that despite his name, the Australian Shepherd hails not from Australia but instead is a relatively recent breed that descends from a probable mix of English, Spanish, and Australian dogs brought to the United States in the early 1800s. Stockmen worked with crosses from these dogs until they ultimately produced a made-in-the-USA dog that became known as the Australian Shepherd.

The Australian Shepherd generally possesses what stockdog workers refer to as a *loose eye* when working. This means that he uses a moderate degree of eye contact to control the herd while moving fairly close and upright, as compared to a *strong-eyed* dog, who stares at the herd from farther away in a lower, crouched position.

it's a
Fact

HIS ANCESTORS ARRIVE

When the American West was still a very wild place in the early 1800s, the eastern United States had many herds of sheep and other livestock that had been brought over from European countries with the people settling this land. Along with the herds came herding dogs, including breeds such as the English Shepherd, Dorset Blue Shag, Scottish Collie, Smithfield Sheepdog, Cumberland Sheepdog, and more. In addition to these breeds came dogs accompanying their people from Spain, Germany, and Australia.

Because conditions in the eastern United States closely resembled those of Europe, the dogs and sheep imported from these areas did well. The ranchers and farmers using the various breeds interbred the best working dogs until the offspring were referred to as simply "collie dogs" or "shepherds," sometimes with reference to their country of origin. Thus, the name "English Shepherd" might refer to any English herding dog rather than to the actual breed, further clouding the Australian Shepherd's origins.

Did You Know? The Australian Shepherd's hallmark short tail sometimes occurs naturally but usually must be docked, or cut, to the accepted length of less than 4 inches. Though it is said that puppies of two to three days old, the age at which docking is done, do not appear to be in pain during the procedure, docking has been outlawed in many countries and is under fire in the United States.

The fact that so many herding dogs entered the United States around the same time also accounts for the confusion about the Aussie's origins. Some people believe that dogs called German Tigers contributed greatly to the Aussie's gene pool, whereas others credit mainly the Spanish dogs brought into this country by the Basque shepherds emigrating from the Pyrenees Mountains between Spain and France, some directly and some after settling for a time in Australia.

In the meantime, a few Spanish and Basque settlers found their way to the western United States, where conditions were hot and arid, with rougher terrain of varying altitudes. There, dogs and sheep were selected for their ability to withstand the harsh weather and landscape, but their numbers remained small until the famous California Gold Rush of the mid-1800s that brought Easterners, Midwesterners, and folks from other countries to the West in hopes of striking it rich.

As California welcomed the vast number and assortment of people, the need for supplies, including mutton, wool, and other livestock, greatly increased. Thus, shepherds drove their flocks west with the help of their eastern-bred and -acclimated dogs. Though hardy animals, these dogs were not ideal for their new environment, so the arriving shepherds sought to improve their dogs' suitability to the land by crossing them with local dogs or with imports from Australia.

SHAPING A BREED

The advent of the Gold Rush marked the beginning of the Australian Shepherd's true origins. Shepherds and stockmen over time interbred dogs that were better suited to the shifting climate and topography of

NOTABLE & QUOTABLE

The Aussie is an energetic breed whose energy can be easily channeled into constructive pursuits. Give your Aussie a job to do, and the energy level will be very manageable. The job can be anything from chasing a ball to running agility to herding, or even just going for long walks or runs with you.

—Cec Connair, Australian Shepherd breeder, trainer, and canine-sport competitor from Baltimore, Ohio

the West; they wanted assertive dogs who were capable of handling different stock and able to think for themselves when needed, but who would still respond readily to commands in the same way as the dogs they had always valued.

Gradually, these dogs took on a certain appearance and easily recognized type that was identified by the misnomer "Australian Shepherd." Why the breed became known as Australian when it was developed in the United States remains one of those enticing historical mysteries, one that various Aussie fanciers have sought to answer but without complete success.

Many conclude that those Basque shepherds who came to the United States by way of Australia brought dogs that were widely used in the Aussie's creation and that this influence accounts for the name. Others feel that the Australian immigrants' dogs brought in during the mid-1800s were largely merle colored, and thus any merle dogs, like those commonly found throughout the breed's history, became associated with Australia.

Whatever the real explanation, the Australian Shepherd of today owes his origins to the tough dogs who worked in the wild, wild West. But such a dog was not destined to remain in a relatively small part of the country, and as people saw these dogs work, admired their intelligence, and marveled at their agility, sooner or later someone was bound to show them to the world. Along came a man by the name of Jay Sisler to do just that.

THE RODEO AND BEYOND

While recovering from an ankle injury, rancher Jay Sisler decided to pass the time by training a litter of Aussie puppies who had been born on his family farm. As it turned out, Sisler had a true natural talent for working with dogs. Even by today's standards, some of the tricks he taught those Aussies—such as playing leapfrog, balancing on a lifted pole, doing handstands, and jumping rope—can make anyone shake his or her head in wonder and amazement.

Leaving their Idaho ranch to take their act on the road, Sisler and the dogs became a favorite with the touring rodeos of the 1950s and 1960s. Though Sisler included a remarkable Greyhound in his act as well, the Aussies were the heart of the performance, and many a spectator left the show determined to own one of these incredible dogs.

The real publicity for the breed arrived when Sisler's later dogs became screen stars in the Disney films *Run, Appaloosa, Run* and *Stub: The Best Cowdog in the West*. The latter film, which featured the characters of the popular television series of the same name, shows Sisler and his dogs in action, performing tricks and working stock. The film, originally aired in the 1970s, was released on DVD in 2008, and many of its fans find it a fun and educational way to explore the Aussie's colorful past.

As usual, when movies or television shows highlight a particular breed, demand increases for that breed. The Aussie became desirable as a pet, and the breed's days as strictly working dogs were left behind. There's no doubt that Sisler's dogs advanced the breed's popularity, and many of today's Aussies are descendants of the dogs used in his performances.

THE ASCA AND THE AKC

In 1957, the Australian Shepherd Club of America (ASCA) was formed by a group of breed fanciers with an interest in preserving the Aussie as a versatile breed that retained its original stockdog work ethic and ability. At that time, however, the registering body was the also recently formed National Stock Dog Registry (NSDR), an organization that focused on working stockdogs.

As interest in herding dwindled or access to livestock disappeared, it became evident that other suitable outlets for the breed's energy and drive should be promoted. In 1971, the ASCA took over the breed registry and started offering competitions that awarded titles in obedience, conformation, tracking, and stockdog work. Today, agility and rally have joined the club's list of titling events.

During the 1980s, some Aussie fanciers pushed for the parent club to seek recognition with the American Kennel Club (AKC), the country's oldest registry for purebred dogs. This move was nixed by the ASCA out of fear that the Australian Shepherd would become more of a show dog than a working or performance dog, a fate that had befallen other breeds. Those in favor of AKC recognition argued that the breed's future rested with the breeders, not with the organization that registered their dogs.

To achieve AKC recognition, the latter group of fanciers formed the United States Australian Shepherd Association (USASA), gaining both AKC affiliation and breed recognition in 1991. Though these people felt that AKC recognition would benefit the breed, dissenters worried that puppies advertised as AKC-registered would increase the breed's popularity to the point that indiscriminate breeders would find producing and selling Aussie puppies to be profitable. Another drawback to breed popularity is that a working dog like the Aussie is a good match for far fewer homes than many other breeds, which means that the

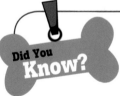

Did You Know? Native Americans purportedly called the Australian Shepherd the "ghost-eyed dog" in reference to the stunning and rather haunting blue eyes frequently seen in the breed, and they are said to have considered such dogs sacred. For this reason, Native Americans allowed anyone traveling their land with a ghost-eyed dog to pass through unharmed.

Teaching your Aussie some fun tricks to show off around the neighborhood or at various animal-charity fundraisers is a wonderful way to provide mental exercise while allowing you an opportunity to learn more about your particular dog's mindset and what motivates him to perform, be it quiet praise, a thrown ball, or a tasty treat.

more Aussie puppies produced, the more that end up in imperfect homes and are eventually surrendered to breed rescues or animal shelters or are shifted around from home to home, often suffering neglect. Fewer litters equal fewer problems.

Fortunately, a growing number of potential owners are educating themselves about the breed before acquiring Aussies. Once people understand the breed's history as a working dog—that it was bred for generations to herd sheep or cattle for days on end in all weather and on rough terrain—it can give pause to those who might otherwise have purchased an Australian Shepherd for the breed's beauty or brains without realizing what they were getting into. On the other hand, such knowledge can inspire those who truly want an active canine partner like the Aussie.

FAME AND FORTUNE

We've mentioned Jay Sisler and his Aussies, but it would be remiss not to talk a little more about his most famous dogs. Littermates Stub and Shorty, plus a female Aussie named Queenie—the stars of the *Stub* television show—were the dogs who started it all. If ever it could be said that three dogs launched a breed's popularity, Stub, Shorty, and Queenie would be those dogs.

Originally trained mainly for the fun of it, these smart dogs took to performing so well that Sisler continued their training, coming up with a repertoire of creative and often humorous tricks. Eventually, these dogs went with Sisler on the rodeo circuit, where they wowed audiences by jumping rope, often two of them at a time; walking on two legs, both front and back; and doing spins, tumbles, balancing feats, and much more.

During their training, Stub, Shorty and Queenie worked initially for praise and, surprisingly, pancakes, though in time the pancakes were put away. Sisler continued to praise them throughout their training, and the dogs delighted in showing off what they'd learned and in pleasing Sisler—to the point that they sometimes got a bit competitive about which dog got to perform which trick.

Despite their busy performance lives, these were real ranch dogs who also knew how to work stock and frequently just

it's a Fact

One of the most influential sires in the history of the breed was Wildhagen's Dutchman of Flintridge, the Australian Shepherd Club of America's first champion of record and the first to earn the Companion Dog (CD) and Companion Dog Excellent (CDX) titles in obedience, all accomplished in 1971.

The breed's herding instinct and desire to work is present even in young puppies.

I used to think it was the stock that turned the drive on in my Aussies, but when one of the puppies I sold excelled in agility, I learned that it's not the stock, it's whatever task they work on with their owners.

—Terry Martin, stockdog worker and breeder from Hico, Texas

hung out with Sisler at their home in Emmett, Idaho. Also used as breeding dogs, they and their descendants appear in many a modern Aussie's pedigree; in fact, Shorty sired a dog by the name of Wood's Jay, who became a well-known and influential early sire and was owned by pioneer breeder Fletcher Wood.

The Aussie's intelligence shines in his sparkling eyes.

These grand beginnings paved the way for other Australian Shepherds to amaze spectators with their earth-defying leaps and remarkable feats of agility—dogs such as Elden McIntire's Hyper Hank, a well-known disc dog (or, as it's better known, Frisbee dog). Hyper Hank performed at several national events during the 1970s, including Super Bowl XII, and made a trip to the White House to perform on the lawn for President Jimmy Carter.

Since these early days of the breed, countless Australian Shepherds have gone on to impress audiences; earn top-level titles in obedience, agility, rally, and other sports; win herding and stockdog trials; work as stockdogs on ranches and farms; and, most of all, become beloved companions for people who want nothing more than a dog who enjoys being active and having fun with his owners.

From the Old West to ranches across America to the big screen and fame (and occasionally fortune), the Aussie has undergone quite a journey in his relatively short existence as an established breed. Perhaps most amazing is that during its travels, the breed has largely retained its working heritage, temperament, and abilities, thanks in part to the breeders who knew this great dog in his early days and were determined not to lose what those before them had created. As most fanciers would agree, it would be difficult to improve upon the Australian Shepherd of old, a fact still being proven today.

The Australian Shepherd of today is equally at home working stock, competing in sports, or entertaining his owners.

You have an unbreakable bond with your dog, but do you always understand him? Go online and download "Dog Speak," which outlines how dogs communicate. Find out what your Australian Shepherd is saying when he barks, howls, or growls. Go to **DogChannel.com/Club-Aussie** and click on "Downloads."

A Child's Companion

Parents often marvel at the bond that develops between their children and their dogs, and breeder Terry Martin of Slash V Working Australian Shepherds in Hico, Texas, is no exception. "From the beginning, my three-year-old son, Randy, decided that this timid puppy who wouldn't come out from under the doghouse was his. He would crawl under there and bring her out, only to watch her scramble back the minute he let go," says Martin.

Knowing that this timid puppy was not a choice pick, Martin encouraged her son to choose a red merle puppy. Red merle was a rare color in those days, and this was the first of the color that Martin's dogs had produced. "I even put the timid puppy in the barn and told Randy that we had sold her, and I brought the red into the house." Nothing doing for Randy, who cried for two days about his lost puppy until finally Martin relented and brought her back to him.

Martin decided to try socializing Randy's "Buster Brown Shoe" puppy, as he called her, and brought her into the house. The terrified puppy hid when she was loose in the house and spent the nights on Randy's bed, afraid to move. Yet the immediate bond that the boy had felt for Buster never faltered. Martin, on the other hand, became frustrated when the fearful puppy ignored her calls but responded the instant Randy called her.

Two years later, Buster had not gone beyond her backyard when Martin made the decision to see what the dog would do when taken around the seventy-five calves that they needed to push through a chute for medical treatment. After watching for a few moments, Buster went to work, helping push the calves through and into the next pen after treatment. Apparently, Buster's genetics had kicked in, and she loved working after that.

"Then, another strange thing happened," says Martin. "Buster did a complete turnaround and became friendly with family and friends. Maybe it was because working those cattle made her feel as if she had control, and that gave her confidence. I'm not sure why, but it was definitely a life-changing experience for her." Buster even started coming into the house when Martin called her.

A puppy of the 1970s, Buster went on to live a long, happy life after her enlightenment and always remained devoted to Randy—and him to her. Martin remembers Buster as her son's constant friend and confidant, a child's irreplaceable companion who will never be forgotten.

Once you've decided that the Australian Shepherd fits your lifestyle and that you fit his, the search begins for the perfect dog. This means that more decisions must be made. Do you want to buy from a breeder or adopt from a rescue? Should you raise a young puppy, find an already house-trained adolescent, or look for a more settled, mannerly adult? Answering these and other questions before starting your quest helps assure a good match.

Let's assume that you want a young puppy, one you can raise to become respectful and loving around your family and your other pets. Obviously, you are seeking a healthy, good-tempered puppy who can join you in the numerous activities you've planned for your energetic canine family member. Finding such a puppy requires reasonable expectations, patience, effort, and some knowledge about what to look for.

Neither the Australian Shepherd Club of America nor the American Kennel Club breed standard lists average weights for the breed; both standards list only height ranges of 18 to 23 inches. For those wondering, males usually weigh somewhere in the range of 50 to 65 pounds, whereas females generally weigh from 40 to 55 pounds.

it's a Fact

First, understand that you're not going to happen upon a well-bred, healthy Australian Shepherd outside your local hardware store or supermarket. In the unlikely event that you find Aussie pups being sold in such a manner, you must steel yourself against the temptation to take one home. Breeders who put the time, effort, and money into producing puppies from genetically sound parents that likewise have great temperament, health, and structure place their puppies with care and forethought.

Buying a puppy from a reputable breeder can cost more than buying from a well-intentioned owner who bred his or her beloved pet despite health issues, but the benefits of buying from a good breeder prove well worth any additional cost. Those who spend less initially on a puppy from non-health-tested parents often suffer the added expense later—not to mention the heartbreak—of repeated trips to the veterinarian for health problems that may or may not be treatable.

On the other hand, a higher price doesn't always indicate superior breeding. This is where you need to do your research so that you know what you are paying for. To help you differentiate the good breeder from the bad, plan to visit the puppies in their home environment so you can see for yourself where they eat, sleep, and play. This will give you the chance to meet the mother, and possibly the father, of the litter while you observe the overall cleanliness of the puppies and their living environment. You are looking for a breeder who feeds nutritious food, raises the puppies in the home where they receive daily human attention, and keeps pups and mom clean, free of parasites, and vaccinated. A breeder who refuses to allow potential puppy buyers to visit the litter has something to hide.

QUESTIONS AND ANSWERS

Begin your search for caring breeders by contacting the Australian Shepherd Club of America (ASCA) or the United States Australian Shepherd Association (USASA), the latter being the American Kennel Club (AKC) parent club for the breed. A local Australian Shepherd club or all-breed kennel club might also point you in the right direction. Some clubs require breeders to sign a code of ethics in order to be listed in their breeder referrals.

In the meantime, make a list of questions to ask each breeder. Ask how long the breeder has owned Aussies. Unless mentored by an experienced breeder, someone who's been in the breed for only a year or so may not know enough about his or her dog's genetic background. A serious breeder studies temperament and health issues for several generations and subsequently chooses breeding pairs that are most likely to have stable, healthy puppies.

Ask how many litters the breeder produces yearly and where the puppies are born and raised. The conscientious

Did You Know?

Breeders, like everyone else, have preferences in what they want in their Aussies, and they breed for those traits. For example, someone who prefers Aussies with friendlier temperaments will likely keep those types of dogs for his or her breeding program. Even so, the genetic tendency toward the breed's more typical reserved nature will come through in some puppies.

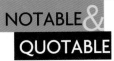

NOTABLE & QUOTABLE

Pups who grow up...with little human contact and little exposure to household items such as phones, doorbells, television, and so on are likely to be fearful of everyday things.

—Sue Pearson, MA, CPDT, owner of Spot & Co. Dog Training in Iowa City, Iowa

breeder who produces one quality litter per year and raises the puppies in the house with lots of attention is preferable to the larger scale breeder with kennels that house several litters at a time. Early attention proves vital to the puppies because frequent daily handling gives them a pleasant association with humans so that they enjoy the touch, smell, and company of new people that they meet. If puppies get too little human attention during those first few weeks, when they are very impressionable, they may forever favor their own kind.

Learn the reason behind the mating that produced the litter, and ask what goals the breeder has in mind for his or her breeding program. A serious breeder readily explains what each parent brings to the plate and what is hoped that the parents will yield in their puppies, be it future conformation stars, top obedience prospects, or great working stockdogs.

Along these lines, both parents should be registered with a well-known purebred registry, such as the AKC, the ASCA, or the United Kennel Club, popular organizations that register the breed and host titling competitions in various canine sports, such as agility, obedience, conformation, and stockdog or herding trials.

One of the most telling questions about a breeder involves what health tests he or she has done on the dogs before breeding them. Health tests cost money—money that those who are into selling puppies strictly for profit won't invest. A breeder who is honestly concerned about the welfare of the parents, puppies, and future owners tests breeding dogs to reduce the risk of the breeding animals' passing any significant health problems on to their young.

For instance, various eye problems can be seen in the Australian Shepherd breed, so both parents' eyes should be certified as normal by a board-certified canine ophthalmologist. This can be done through the Canine Eye Registration Foundation (CERF), an organization that maintains a database of dogs' eye-testing results.

Hip dysplasia, a hip-joint malformation, should also be ruled out through x-ray examination. Two organizations commonly read x-rays, certify hips, and maintain databases of hip scores—the Orthopedic Foundation for Animals (OFA) and the University of Pennsylvania's PennHIP. Some breeders also have their dogs' elbows x-rayed to check elbow formation and rule out elbow dysplasia.

Additionally, ask breeders if epilepsy, allergies, thyroid problems, or other health issues have shown up in their dogs or puppies. Keep in mind that no breed and no bloodline in any breed escapes all health issues. In addition to heredity, factors such as diet, environment, and care affect health. In short, seek a breeder who strives for perfect health in his or her dogs but understand that you won't find anyone who is 100 percent successful.

Did You Know?

Though the Australian Shepherd was ultimately made in America, the breed eventually found its way to the "land down under," where breeders, such as those belonging to the Australian Shepherd Club of Victoria, proudly show, trial, and work their namesake breed in addition to promoting responsible ownership and breeding.

Questions to Expect

Be prepared for the breeder to ask you some questions, too.

JOIN OUR
ONLINE
**Club
Aussie**™

1. Have you previously owned an Australian Shepherd?

The breeder is trying to gauge how familiar you are with the Aussie. If you have never owned one, illustrate your knowledge of the breed by telling the breeder about your research.

2. Do you have children? What are their ages?

Some breeders are wary about selling a puppy to families with younger children.

This isn't a steadfast rule, and some breeders insist on meeting the kids to see how they handle puppies. It all depends on the breeder.

3. How long have you wanted an Aussie?

This helps a breeder know if your purchase is an impulse buy or a carefully thought-out decision. Buying on impulse is one of the biggest mistakes owners can make. Be patient.

Join Club Aussie to get a complete list of questions that a breeder should ask you. Click on "Downloads" at **DogChannel.com/Club-Aussie.**

During your conversations with breeders, take notice of which ones ask as many questions of you as you do of them. After all of the study, work, and care that a good breeder puts into producing quality puppies, you can bet that the breeder will do his or her absolute best to place those puppies in loving homes. The breeder should ask you where you plan to keep the puppy, how and where you plan to exercise him, and what type of training you plan to pursue.

Another important factor to consider when interviewing breeders is how many breeds that person has. Some reputable breeders can knowledgeably and responsibly produce litters from two or perhaps three breeds, but more than that shows a lack of dedication to, and a probable lack of knowledge about, any one breed, and that could result in perpetuating health or temperament problems.

A spay/neuter agreement indicates that a breeder cares about the puppies he or she produces. This requires an owner of a non-conformation/non-breeding Aussie to supply the breeder with proof of spaying or neutering once the puppy reaches an appropriate age. New owners sometimes feel that a breeder oversteps boundaries with such an agreement, but buyers of pet puppies should understand that it helps breeders prevent unscrupulous people from obtaining and breeding their dogs for profit.

Here are a few other benefits of buying from a caring, reputable breeder:

1. A reputable breeder gives references.
2. A reputable breeder provides a small amount of the puppy's food, something with his mom's and littermates' scent to comfort him, his health and vaccination record, and often a breed or training book when you pick your puppy up.

3. A reputable breeder suggests that you take your new puppy to the veterinarian within a few days of purchase for a thorough examination and offers to take the puppy back for a full refund should the doctor find a health problem.
4. A reputable breeder promises support by being available to answer questions and offer informed advice throughout your puppy's life.
5. A reputable breeder reserves the option of taking the puppy or grown dog back if you can no longer care for him or to approve another home if you need to rehome him and know someone who wants to take him. This agreement helps the breeder assure that his or her dogs stay in good homes.

When talking to breeders, it goes without saying that courtesy and responsibility work both ways. Good breeders receive a lot of inquiries into their litters and frequently compile waiting lists of potential puppy buyers. You may need to put down a deposit with the breeder of your choice once you decide on a litter. Generally, you can expect a refund if no puppies within the litter fit your criteria.

Answer the breeder's questions politely and try not to be offended if he or she asks about your home environment, family lifestyle, plans for the puppy, and so on. Even if the breeder thinks that you'll provide a perfect home for an Aussie puppy, the more the breeder learns about your situation, the easier it is for him or her to match you up with the perfect puppy.

PUPPY PARTICULARS

You may have certain preferences when it comes to your future Aussie. You may want one with blue merle coloring, you may love

Tale of Two Aussies

Years ago, Jenn Merritt of Efland, North Carolina, a professional trainer who is certified with the Association of Pet Dog Trainers, received a call from her local shelter about fostering a six-month-old, scrawny, blind "albino," as they called her, Aussie. Merritt says, "I discovered that Lambchop was not albino but a double merle—a mostly white Aussie produced from a merle-to-merle breeding."

Determined to help, Merritt says, "As Lambchop jumped into my lap, with her deformed eyes and pink nose, I had no idea what lay ahead." Merritt found out that Lambchop was originally purchased at the county fairgrounds from someone who sold merle puppies regularly. Merritt also discovered that "Lambchop's blindness was common for double merles, as is deafness and issues with many major organ systems. Over the next six years, my husband and I dealt with the range of Lambchop's health and behavioral issues."

Merritt says, "The most serious and perpetual issue was unpredictable aggression toward our other dogs and eventually toward us, probably exacerbated by neurological abnormalities. Over time, the issues went beyond what she or we could handle." At that point, Lambchop was euthanized as she rested in Merritt's arms on what Merritt says was one of the saddest days of her life.

"When I think of her, I also think about all those other people who went home with double merles and merles...from that one 'breeder' at the county fairgrounds," says Merritt. "No amount of love, gentle training, nutrition, or medical care could replace or mend what Lambchop's body and brain were lacking: genetic health and sound temperament."

Lambchop's lesson hit hard enough that Merritt wanted to "raise and live with an Aussie that had the advantages Lambchop did not, and to know and have the very best of what the breed could be."

"After many months of information-gathering, reading, phone calls, emails, waiting lists, and traveling, we brought home our red-tri puppy, Royal," she says. Royal was bred by a knowledgeable breeder. Merritt says that the breeder also provided excellent nutrition throughout the mom's pregnancy and socialized the puppies to various stimuli up until they went to new homes.

Merritt says, "Royal has been everything we had hoped: robustly healthy, confident, biddable, and simply a joy to live with." Merritt offers the following advice: "Do your homework and search out breeders that make genetic health and temperament their priorities, especially in our favorite breed, where so much can go right or go wrong."

dark-eyed dogs, or you may like the look of a full white collar on an Aussie. If you're willing to wait for a puppy with your aesthetic preferences from a quality breeder, that's fine, but keep in mind that once you own a healthy, well-structured Aussie with a good temperament, he'll soon be the most beautiful dog on earth regardless of coloration, eye shade, or markings.

As for male or female, both sexes make equally good pets. Some people say that females are more affectionate, while others argue that males are more loving. There are people who swear that females are more devoted, whereas the next person insists the same about males. In truth, it really comes down to the individual dog and any preference on your part.

Tell the breeder about any activities you plan to do with your dog. Though Aussie temperament traits tend to be consistent, individual personalities vary. The puppy that constantly plays in the wading pool might make the perfect companion for the owner who spends a lot of time at a lake. The bold puppy that loves climbing over

things might make the best agility prospect. An Australian Shepherd he may be, but your puppy is also unique.

This brings up the subject of who chooses the puppy. A serious breeder studies the puppies and learns a great deal about their personalities during those first few weeks. Because of this, your breeder will probably narrow your choice down to the two or three puppies that he or she feels will suit you best. Although difficult for buyers who envision choosing from an entire litter of adorable puppies, matchmaking advice from the breeder helps ensure that buyers get the puppies of their dreams.

Besides observing the litter and noting individual traits, breeders often do some temperament testing before matching puppies with owners. These tests typically gauge each puppy's reaction to being restrained, desire to be around people, retrieval instinct, touch sensitivity, and more. Only an experienced tester familiar with Aussies should judge the pups' reactions, as there are many factors involved.

If you have to reserve a puppy before the litter is born, visit the breeder's home before putting down a deposit to ensure that the dogs look well cared for and display proper Aussie temperaments. Pay particular attention to the mother-to-be and, if he is on the premises, the litter's dad. Somewhat aloof temperaments are normal, and friendliness is fine, but if either dog acts overtly aggressive, thank the breeder for taking time to see you and continue your search.

Given that a pregnant momma will look a bit heavy, albeit not obese, the breeder's other dogs should display the Aussie's typically lithe, muscular build. Coats should be clean, shiny, and brushed, without strong odor or bare spots. Look for nicely trimmed toenails, grime-free ears, and bright eyes.

it's a Fact

Breeding a merle to another merle carries the risk that 25 percent of the litter will be what are called *homozygous* merles. These predominantly white Aussies often end up blind, deaf, or both, as a byproduct of the gene that accounts for the breed's beautiful merle coloring. Homozygous merles can be avoided by mating merles with solid-colored dogs.

Responsible breeders work to ensure that soundness of body and mind and all of the unique characteristics that make the Aussie what it is are passed down from generation to generation.

JOIN OUR ONLINE **Club Aussie™**

Breeder Q&A

Here are some questions you should ask a breeder and the answers you want.

Q. How often do you have litters available?

A. You want to hear "once or twice a year" or "occasionally" because a breeder who doesn't have litters that often is probably more concerned with the quality of his or her puppies than with making money.

Q. What kinds of health problems do Aussies have?

A. Beware of a breeder who says "none." In Australian Shepherds, some genetic health problems include hip and elbow dysplasia, various eye diseases, and auto-immune illnesses.

Get a complete list of questions to ask an Aussie breeder—and the ideal answers—at Club Aussie. Log onto **DogChannel.com/Club-Aussie** and click on "Downloads."

The breeder's home may show telltale signs of wear from years in dogs, but it should appear relatively clean, without strong doggy or urine odors. If the breeder has outdoor runs for the dogs, these too should be clean and reasonably waste-free. Ask to see where the puppies will be raised inside the home and also note the conditions there. If all looks good and you feel comfortable with this breeder, put down your deposit.

If you are lucky enough to find a quality breeder who has puppies available, this visit becomes much more as you also consider the appearance and condition of the puppies. By the time the breeder allows you to visit a litter, the puppies will probably be at least four to five weeks old. Like mom, they should have clean coats, bright eyes, and be alert, curious—and, at this young age—friendly.

THE FINAL CHOICE

Once the breeder lets you know which puppies meet your needs, the final choice rests with you. Now you can let your intuition guide you or do your own personal evaluations as you watch the puppies interact with each other and with you. Sometimes it works out that you and one certain puppy seem drawn to each other, or it may happen that they all crawl all over you and seem equally adorable, making the choice difficult.

If you have done everything right and worked with the breeder to assure that you and one of these puppies are a good match, then you really can't go wrong in

With such a dazzling array of eye and coat colors, it's hard not to choose an Aussie based on looks alone; however, much more than that must factor into your decision.

your decision. With that in mind, relax, enjoy yourself, play with the puppies for a while, make your choice, and treasure these moments before beginning your new life together with your Australian Shepherd—you will look back on this day with fondness for many years to come.

NO PAPER CHASE

Good breeders keep puppies until they are at least eight weeks old, so when you return to pick up your pup, the breeder should have your puppy's registration papers ready to go. Many breeders provide a copy of a pedigree that shows your puppy's predecessors for three or more generations and includes the names and titles of the dogs that form your puppy's roots. Because you are buying from a conscientious breeder who breeds dogs that conform to the breed standard for the Australian Shepherd and showcase the breed's versatility, a variety of titles probably grace that pedigree.

At this time, you should receive a copy of the contract that outlines the breeder's health guarantee, conditions under which the breeder will take the puppy or adult dog back, spay and neuter requirements, and any other particulars previously agreed upon by both parties. Your breeder will also provide you with your puppy's health record, which lists his birthday and documents the dates on which he received any worming medications and vaccinations. Your veterinarian will want to see this when you take your puppy in for his check-up.

ALTERNATIVES

Keep an open mind during your puppy search. If you contact a good breeder who has an older puppy or a young adult who he or she has raised in the home and feels might fit well with you, consider the possible advantages. This puppy or dog should be fully vaccinated, at least partially house-trained, past the worst of the puppy nipping stage, used to car rides, and much more. For example, an eight-week-old puppy needs a chance to eliminate every hour, plus after meals and upon waking from naps. A five-month-old puppy usually eats twice a day and can wait a few hours between potty trips, which is an easier situation for most owners to handle.

If you have children, you will have to make sure that an older puppy has been around kids quite a bit and likes them. In this case, assuming the puppy or dog has a good basic temperament and has been well socialized by going many places and meeting a variety of people and other dogs, an older puppy holds the same promise as the tiny eight-week-old puppy.

The "more-mature-equals-easier" idea frequently holds true for Aussies taken in by breed rescue groups or animal shelters, with many dogs displaced due to divorces, moving, lost jobs, or other hapless situations that really had nothing to do with

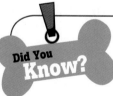

Did You Know? The Australian Shepherd's medium-length, moderately coarse outer coat combined with a close-fitting undercoat that sheds out in warmer seasons was bred into the Aussie for the weatherproofing it provided and because this type of coat casts off dried mud and manure, both valuable assets for a working stockdog.

the dog or his behavior. Oftentimes, these Aussies make wonderful companions, each wanting nothing more than to find a caring family to forever love and watch over.

Other dogs in rescues or in shelters were not fortunate in their first homes and come with what trainers often refer to as "baggage," meaning that these dogs have temperament issues caused by a lack of attention or training, poor breeding, inadequate socialization, abuse, or other precursors. Shyness, separation anxiety, destructive tendencies, and other problems are not uncommon. Many of these issues can be worked on by dedicated owners, but for safety reasons, aggressive dogs are not adopted out.

Some rescue dogs, referred to as "special needs" dogs, suffer health issues caused by injuries, genetics, neglect, or other factors, which vary from permanent conditions to those easily treated. Prospective owners considering special needs dogs should understand exactly what they're taking on and assess their commitment to provide the necessary healthcare.

Adopting a homeless dog with temperament issues requires careful thought. Minor problems, like slight shyness, can usually be corrected with pleasant socialization and training, such as agility, to build the dog's confidence. No matter the problem, unless you have experience with Aussies and with training, enlisting the aid of an experienced professional trainer who is familiar with Australian Shepherds is advisable.

Whether you acquire an eight-week-old puppy, an adolescent or young adult, or an adult Aussie fallen on hard times, that dog depends on you for care, attention, training, exercise, safety, and love. He also needs a strong but fair leader who will show him acceptable behaviors in the household and away from home. Meet these simple needs, and no breed will repay your kindness better than an Australian Shepherd.

Healthy Puppy Signs

Here are a few things you should look for when selecting a puppy from a litter.

1. **NOSE:** It should be slightly moist to the touch, but there shouldn't be excessive discharge. The puppy should not be sneezing or sniffling persistently.

2. **SKIN AND COAT:** Your Aussie puppy's coat should be soft and shiny, without flakes or excessive shedding. Watch out for patches of missing hair, redness, bumps, or sores. The pup should have a pleasant smell. Check for parasites, such as fleas or ticks.

3. **BEHAVIOR:** A healthy Aussie puppy may be sleepy, but he should not be lethargic. A healthy puppy will be playful at times, not isolated in a corner. You should see occasional bursts of energy and interaction with his littermates. When it's mealtime, a healthy puppy will take an interest in his food.

There are other signs to look for when picking out the perfect Aussie puppy for your lifestyle. Download the list at **DogChannel.com/Club-Aussie.**

The most important part about getting a new puppy is patience. Plan well in advance for your new family member. Many breeders have waiting lists, and you may not get to choose your pup. Breeders often are breeding for themselves, but what they want may not be what you want. There are many "picks" in a litter.

—Mindy Mymudes, a trainer from Milwaukee, Wisconsin

Nothing looks cuter than an Aussie puppy playfully scurrying off with a roll of paper towels or bravely ambushing the cat statue in the corner, but for your sake and his, store these and other items safely out of reach. Puppies and young adolescent dogs can find trouble the second you turn your back unless you puppy-proof their surroundings by removing, locking away, or putting out of reach any potential hazards.

Much like we touch things with our hands, puppies explore their world largely with their mouths. A seemingly innocuous item can cause monumental problems if your puppy does more than just touch and goes on to ingest it. He could end up with serious digestive troubles or even a blockage that requires surgery, a situation better

Puppies eat weird things, such as socks, underwear, rocks, toys, and more, that can result in serious intestinal blockages that require emergency surgery. A combination of giving the puppy enough exercise, supervising him, keeping things out of reach, and teaching a reliable *leave it* cue offers the most successful preventative measures. Called *pica* when exhibited in adult dogs, most puppies thankfully outgrow this habit of eating non-food items.

it's a
Fact

prevented than dealt with after the fact. To be proactive, smart owners think several steps ahead of their puppy.

PUPPY-PROOFING

Before your Australian Shepherd puppy comes home, choose one or two areas to be his "romper room" and puppy-proof those areas rather than tackling the entire house. Limiting your puppy's initial freedom to a designated area allows him to feel safe and secure far more quickly than if he were allowed run of the entire home, which can seem like a huge, scary place to a new puppy. House-training can also progress much faster when your Aussie learns to keep his home clean one area at a time rather than being expected to "hold it" throughout the house.

In addition to using his mouth to touch and hold, your puppy will need to chew. Chewing provides an enjoyable pastime; soothes his gums, which are sore from teething; and, to your benefit, keeps the little one busy and contented. Provide suitable chew toys, such as durable nylon bones, rubber toys that you can fill with food, or some other type of safe, sturdy chew toy. Never give your puppy an old shoe or another household item to chew on because he cannot tell the difference between his worn-out loafer and your brand-new Prada pumps, and he will think that his teeth have free rein.

In your puppy's romper room, bend down to puppy level and take a look around. You might be surprised at what you see: electrical cords, a magazine holder, a tasseled rug, laundry in a basket, and more. Exposed electrical cords must be covered with chew-proof guards, which are sold in pet-supply or hardware stores. Many people use outlet inserts in unused outlets, though this can backfire if the puppy notices them and tries to chew on them.

Remove items such as magazines, newspapers, figurines, and anything else chewable or breakable that might be within your Aussie's reach. Laundry may not seem like a hazard, but countless puppies have died or have needed life-saving surgery after swallowing a sock or another piece of clothing.

Detergent, fabric softener, and dryer sheets, as well as any other chemical-based items, such as household cleaning products, should be locked away, far out of puppy's reach. Never assume that your Aussie won't ingest something because we consider it inedible. Antifreeze is a common killer of puppies and dogs, who apparently like the chemical's sweet taste. On the other hand, certain foods that humans enjoy—including chocolate, raisins, grapes, macadamia nuts, and onions—are dangerous to dogs. Regarding chocolate, darker chocolate is worse for dogs, and baking chocolate is particularly toxic.

Did You Know? **Just as a too-tired child becomes a little grumpy, an over-tired puppy sometimes acts his naughtiest,** evidenced by extreme nipping, getting into things, and other annoying behaviors, because he needs a nap. If your puppy "acts up" despite adequate exercise and attention, calm him down with a safe chew or a treat-stuffed rubber toy, and he'll probably fall right to sleep.

In addition to love and attention, you need to provide your Aussie with a safe home.

For your two- to five-month old teething Aussie puppy, purchase a safe chew toy that also relieves some teething pain. A freezable chew toy will soothe sore gums by numbing them with cold while still providing the massage your puppy craves.

Safety rules also apply when enjoying the great outdoors with your puppy. Keep chemicals safely away from your puppy's reach and do not use fertilizers or other lawn treatments in areas where your puppy will play. Cocoa mulches and colored mulches present edible hazards that are potentially toxic or capable of causing internal blockages. Many dogs will graze on grass, but they should be discouraged from munching on decorative plants, as many types (such as azalea and yew) can cause serious adverse reactions or even death if ingested.

Keep in mind during this stage of development that your young Aussie never chews something "out of spite" or "because he's mad." Remember, puppies chew because it is natural for them and to alleviate the gum pain that accompanies teething. If your Aussie chews something he shouldn't, quietly tell him "Uh-uh" and offer him a suitable replacement chew as you gently take the forbidden item away. Then scold yourself for not paying better attention and promise to do better next time.

Every owner must be aware that no amount of puppy-proofing can keep a loose, unsupervised Aussie safe. A bored, lonely, or upset puppy might literally eat through drywall, chew up the baseboard, pull off the wallpaper, or commit some equally unexpected and damaging deed. The young puppy or adolescent has no idea that you don't approve of his actions; he just needs a diversion to keep him busy, and he will find something in his surroundings to alleviate his boredom.

"A tired puppy is a good puppy"—a common saying among dog trainers—rings true because ensuring that your Aussie youngster receives adequate attention and exercise will help prevent him from engaging in destructive behaviors. However, nothing guarantees that your puppy will not suddenly decide to pull that fuzzy string sticking up from the carpet and keep pulling. Averting this type of behavior requires supervision and safe, comfortable confinement when needed.

When your Aussie puppy is loose in the home or yard, under your supervision, he needs your guidance to learn what you consider acceptable and unacceptable behavior. For those times when you cannot provide that supervision, give your puppy a refuge that keeps him out of mischief. Crates are very popular for this purpose. You can use one of the many styles of wire or plastic crates in an appropriate size for your Australian Shepherd. Place the crate in a draft-free area of the home where he can watch the family members going about their business, giving him the security of knowing that someone is there.

Choosing suitable bedding for a puppy can be tricky, as you don't want your pup chewing it up and possibly swallowing pieces of it. Many companies make chew-resistant beds that prove particularly effective for young puppies. It helps to buy a bed with a zippered cover so that you can insert a small towel or cloth with his mom's and littermates' scent to give the little one a bit of comfort in his new home.

Dropped pills often bounce into corners where a vacuum doesn't reach but a curious puppy can lick them up. Always find or clean up dropped or spilled medication immediately, supervise your puppy closely when visiting friends' homes, and inspect any hotel rooms where you stay. If your puppy ingests a potentially poisonous medication (or any potentially dangerous item), call your veterinarian or call the ASPCA's poison-control hotline at 888-426-4435 (there is a fee for this service).

MEET THE FAMILY

You have your puppy's area prepared and his crate ready, and you are looking forward to watching him discover his new world. The time has come to bring your Australian Shepherd home. Limit your puppy's first few days to time with you and the family while he explores his surroundings and becomes more secure in his new home environment. There will be plenty of time to check out the neighborhood after he has settled in for a few days.

Remind yourself that as bold as your puppy may have been at the breeder's house, leaving his littermates, his mom, and his former family is a very scary experience. After leaving them, he had to ride in an unfamiliar vehicle with someone he barely knows, enter a home he's never seen, and then, if his new owners are a family, meet several more new people. To lessen his anxiety, don't let the entire family crowd around him as soon as he walks in the door. Give him some quiet time to look around and then let him rest before introducing the family.

Young children should not pick up the puppy, as dropping him could cause serious injury. Of course, any children in the family will want to pet the new puppy, so help them sit on the floor and gently handle and caress the baby Aussie. Encourage quiet interaction; do not allow puppy and child to chase each other, but let them simply follow one another around as they develop a bond and discover the wonders of the world together.

Introductions to other pets within the household should be approached carefully, particularly if those pets have never had another dog sharing their home. A puppy-friendly adult dog may welcome the new Aussie with playful antics, but a dog who is less fond of puppies might not appreciate the youngster's lack of manners and sharp teeth. Always supervise interactions and respect the older dog's space by giving him a clear path to get away from the puppy. It is hoped that they will become fast friends, but you should realize that is not always the case.

The family cat will usually be the least appreciative of a new puppy unless you happen to own a very dog-friendly feline. A friendly feline will usually just swat at a puppy with her claws retracted to back him off and teach him a valuable lesson in respect. Make sure that your cat always has ample egress from the puppy to prevent the pup from sustaining a nasty scratch or bite. Never allow the puppy to chase or jump at the cat.

Other pets, such as hamsters, gerbils, rabbits, and other small mammals, will be at risk around a playful Australian Shepherd puppy or, in time, a prey-driven adolescent. Prey drive relates to the canine instinct to

Your on-the-go Aussie puppy will want to explore and play in his new environment.

chase and grab when hunting, and it correlates directly to the herding dog's working instinct. In other words, the herding instinct manifests as a controlled prey drive that kicks in as your puppy matures and can prompt him to go after small animals.

Puppies play hard, fall asleep in a flash, and nap often. When your puppy snuggles in for a nap, make sure that the family members let him rest. Your eight-week-old puppy will sleep frequently throughout the day, and he needs this down time to stay happy and healthy. Some owners find it easier to set a family rule that the puppy is never to be disturbed in his crate, and they put the Aussie in his crate for all naptimes and mealtimes.

NIGHT-NIGHT TIME

After all of the excitement of his first day at home, you may feel sure that your puppy will settle contentedly into that soft bed in his secure crate and sleep through the night. Only on rare occasions does this happen. Understand that your puppy misses the warmth and familiarity of his mom and littermates and the breeder's home, and once the day's fun has ended, that loneliness and uncertainty will likely overwhelm him.

Most puppies do not hold back their feelings, and yours might spend much of his first night whining, crying, barking, and otherwise vocalizing his melancholy. Puppies younger than three months usually need to go out to potty at least once during an eight-hour night, but other than when taking him outside, do not let your Aussie out of his crate at night to comfort him, or he will quickly learn that whining gets him the attention he wants. Along the same lines, do not chastise him for expressing his feelings—he cannot help it!

Some puppies find it comforting to be in the same room where their new people sleep. Your pup may settle down better if his crate is next to your bed, but don't plan on a full night's rest, as he will no doubt still whine quite a bit during the first night. His vocalizations should lessen each night as he realizes that you will take care of him and his feeling of security increases. Just remember, do not encourage his whining by giving in those first few nights.

If you don't want your pup's crate in your bedroom permanently, consider using two crates initially. As your Aussie becomes comfortable in your home and in the crate that you use for daytime naps, he will eventually be content in that crate at night as well. Should you choose to crate him somewhere other than your bedroom from the

Some ordinary household items make great toys for your Aussie—as long you make sure that they are safe. Tennis balls, plastic water bottles, old towels, and more can be transformed into fun with a little creativity. You can find a list of home-made toys at **DogChannel.com/Club-Aussie.**

JOIN OUR ONLINE Club Aussie™

Fabric crates that fold down for easy carrying work great for traveling with an adult Aussie that behaves nicely in his crate, but a rowdy puppy can easily chew through the fabric, rip the zipper, or roll this lightweight crate over. Stick with a sturdy wire or plastic crate for use both at home and on the road.

pulsed in his ear as he cuddled with them in his former home, and a warm (not hot) water bottle placed under the puppy's bed simulates their body warmth. Alternatively, many pet-supply stores sell cuddly toys that warm up and mimic the canine heartbeat to help comfort young puppies. As previously mentioned, you can place a cloth from the breeder's home with the scent of your puppy's mom and siblings inside his bed.

Check frequently to make sure that your Aussie doesn't chew any of these comfort items; chewing becomes more likely as he settles in and starts looking for things to keep him busy in his crate. When he starts to chew, remove the comfort aids and provide only safe chew toys in his crate.

start, his vocalizing may be more intense at first, but he should settle down pretty nicely within a week. Sometimes playing a radio tuned to soft music or a talk show calms the puppy when he cannot hear you.

A traditional trick is to place a loudly ticking clock next to the puppy's crate or under his bed. The comforting tick-tock cadence resembles the rhythmic sound of his mom's and siblings' heartbeats that

SHOPPING LIST

Let's review some of the previously mentioned puppy supplies and take a look at additional items that you might find nec-

A comfortable bed will give your Australian Shepherd a cozy place to snuggle up.

Collars, leashes, and ID tags are among the gear needed for your Aussie's homecoming.

One thing owners need to keep in mind is the puppy's view as seen from [the puppy's] height. We look at everything from above the puppy, but we need to puppy-proof from puppy level because puppies' view of the world is much lower than ours.

—Jean M. Burton, Australian Shepherd fancier and owner of Desert Dog Obedience in Phoenix, Arizona

Rather than let your energetic puppy immediately rush up to your resident dog, keep them apart for a few days to give your older dog time to adapt to the newcomer's presence around the house and yard. After such an adjustment period, allow a carefully supervised introduction.

essary or convenient. Obviously, one of your major purchases will be your puppy's crate. Buy a sturdy plastic or wire crate rather than a soft canvas style; the latter type is too easily destroyed by a youngster with a penchant for chewing on or pawing at his crate. A sturdily made crate can last your Aussie's entire lifetime.

The crate should fit your Australian Shepherd as an adult, meaning that when full grown, he should be able to stand up, turn around, and stretch out inside. Some stores sell crate dividers or partitions to create a puppy-sized space in an adult-sized crate. The intent is to initially give the puppy a smaller space to encourage him not to relieve himself in his crate. This principle is based on the fact that this naturally clean animal won't want to lie in his mess, but some argue that a puppy should not be forced to hold it that long. The bottom line is that your puppy must go outside frequently and regularly for potty breaks and shouldn't be left in his crate so long that he becomes uncomfortable.

Bedding should be soft, washable, suitably sized for the crate, and preferably chew resistant, though the latter may not be necessary unless your puppy shows destructive tendencies. If you happen to be handy with a needle and thread, consider making your own dog bed, which is a relatively easy task for someone with basic sewing knowledge.

The reputable breeder from whom you acquire your Australian Shepherd will no doubt send a small supply of your puppy's current food home with you, but do your own research before choosing a specific brand or type of food to use long term. Countless commercial diets, ranging from kibble to canned food to raw food, can be found in pet-supply stores, with some diets better than others. For the health of your dog, do your homework and find a good-quality food that your Aussie likes before stocking up.

Everyone enjoys buying toys for their dogs, a fact well documented by the plethora of toys available for purchase. Safe chew bones, sturdy toys made of rubber or other synthetic materials, and treat-filled or treat-dispensing toys make fine play items that will keep your Aussie occupied. Soft stuffed toys are suitable for some puppies, while other puppies start pulling or chewing on threads, eyeballs, or ears almost immediately, destroying the toys and creating choking hazards, which puts such toys into the "under-supervision-only" category.

Be sure to buy a leash and an adjustable collar, preferably with your phone number embroidered onto the collar, along with an identification tag and a license tag to help ensure your puppy's return should he somehow escape. Other necessary supplies include food and water bowls and doggy (or baby) gates for blocking access to off-limits areas. Cleaning products designed to neutralize odors and remove stains from carpeting and other surfaces will undoubtedly prove essential until your puppy is house-trained.

If your home has a swimming pool, teach your dog how to exit. Dogs tend to go to the side of any body of water to get out. Many dogs cannot pull themselves over the side of the pool walls and, if not taught how to get to the steps, may hang on the side of the pool until they fatigue and potentially drown.

—Nicole Kelly, emergency veterinary technician from Tucson, Arizona

H ouse-training issues remain among the top reasons for owners' surrendering puppies and dogs to shelters or rescues. The fact is that many people set their puppies up for failure by allowing too much freedom too soon, offering inadequate supervision, not keeping to suitable schedules, and failing to utilize crates properly. As a smart Australian Shepherd owner, you must learn to avoid common pitfalls and efficiently house-train your puppy with as few accidents as "caninely" possible.

An important point for every new dog owner to keep in mind is the frequency with which puppies eliminate. The younger the puppy, the more often he eats and drinks, the smaller his excretory system is, and the less control he has over those organs. For instance, a typical eight- to twelve-week-old Aussie needs the chance to relieve himself every one to two hours during active daytime hours and at least

Initially keeping your Aussie puppy in the room where the outside potty door is located helps him learn to tell you that he needs to go by running to the nearby door. Conversely, expecting your young puppy to negotiate a maze of rooms in order to run to that important door will probably result in an accident before he finds his way.

it's a Fact

once during the quiet of the night, a schedule that most owners underestimate.

For owners who work outside the home, this proves to be a difficult or even impossible schedule. In cases like this, many trainers recommend adopting a slightly older puppy. For those who work and really want to start with a young puppy, enlisting the aid of neighbors, friends, dog walkers, or other helpers will be necessary to ensure that the puppy can get outside as often as he needs to. Otherwise, he may be forced to eliminate in his crate, a behavior that this naturally clean animal will try to avoid unless repeatedly given no other option.

House-training is necessary for a harmonious relationship with your Aussie in your home.

SETTING UP FOR SUCCESS

Start by choosing a specific potty area. Both the familiarity and residual smell of a consistent spot helps cue your puppy to what he's supposed to do.

Decide right away on a verbal cue for each eliminative function, such as "Pee" or "Potty" for urination and "Do your business," or the more direct "Go poop" for defecation. Using a separate cue for each gives you the ability to remind the playful puppy who just did one or the other that he still has unfinished business and that he should stop chasing butterflies long enough to finish up before he goes back inside the house.

Unless you know that your puppy urgently needs to go, encourage him to walk with you to the door leading outside to his potty area. This teaches him how to find the correct exit so that in time he will automatically run to that door when he needs to go outside, thus alerting you to take him out before he has an accident. Some owners even put a hanging bell on the door and teach the puppy to ring the bell as an alert.

Before your puppy learns to alert you about going outside, notice what body-language signs reveal that he needs to relieve himself. Common indicators include pacing, whining,

Puppies need supervision 24/7. One way to facilitate this is to strategically locate puppy playpens in areas where the family congregates. In this way, the puppy is confined yet near the family and has access to only his toys and area.

—Jean Burton, nationally ranked Australian Shepherd Club of America obedience competitor from Phoenix, Arizona

Whether to allow your Aussie on your furniture is a personal choice, but be careful about allowing your little puppy to fall asleep on the couch, as you'll have to be very watchful when she wakes up. Puppies usually need to urinate immediately after waking up from naps, and the not-yet-house-trained puppy doesn't know not to soil the couch.

looking quickly around the room, circling, and, of course, starting to squat; all of these are signals telling you to take your puppy out *now*. If you catch him mid-squat, saying a gentle "No" or "Uh-uh" provides important "that's not what I want" feedback without scaring or hurting him.

Never hit your puppy with your hand, a rolled-up newspaper, or anything else if he has an accident indoors. Punishment is not only unnecessary but it also often creates other problems. For example, the puppy may not understand that he's being punished for eliminating indoors and may think that he's being punished simply for the act of peeing or pooping. In his attempt to not upset you, he simply learns to hide to relieve himself rather than alerting you when he needs to go outside.

Rather than focus on when your puppy makes a mistake, concentrate on teaching him what you do want by rewarding him generously with praise and a treat imme-diately after he potties outside. Sometimes owners make the mistake of waiting to give the puppy a treat until they bring him inside, with the result that the puppy thinks that coming into the house is what earns him the reward. This incorrect conclusion often prompts him to rush around outside without doing his business because he's excited to get his "coming-back-in" treat.

Because your puppy has an attention span of only a few seconds, and he there-fore becomes easily distracted when out-side, always watch to make sure that he actually goes before you take him back into the house. Trainers often hear owners say, "He waited until he came back in to go." Some owners erroneously think that the puppy is acting out of spite, but really the little one simply loses focus on the task at hand amid the excitement of being out-doors and then is physically reminded that he has to go once away from such stimuli.

Taking your puppy outside on leash gives you some control over his wander-ing attention in that it prevents him from running after birds, digging for worms, or pursuing other fascinating endeavors. Once he finishes his business, an off-leash play session in your safely fenced yard is fine and makes a nice reward. Even if you go directly into the house after he goes, play with your puppy for a few min-utes. Don't regularly rush your Australian Shepherd into his crate after he potties, or he will avoid doing his business to avoid the ensuing confinement.

If furniture is off limits, please do not ever allow Rover access [to it]. When he is a puppy, be sure to sit on the floor with him. Some folks think that holding a puppy on their laps has nothing to do with teaching him to be on the sofa. Just remember, if that lap is on the sofa, so is Rover.

—Maggie Blutreich, a certified professional dog trainer and owner of BRAVO!
Force Free Training near Charlotte, North Carolina

Setting up your puppy's romper room as described in the discussion on puppy-proofing (see chapter 4) precludes you from needing to remove unsafe objects from the entire home and offers the added benefit of reducing the size of the area in which your puppy can have accidents. This limited space also makes it easier for him to respect the area as his own, which will encourage him to keep it clean and to learn where the outside door is located.

The puppy's freedom can be increased as he matures and develops more control over his eliminative organs but should be introduced one room at a time. Owners often think that because their puppy does well in his usual area that he understands not to potty indoors in general. In actuality, he must be taught to extend his clean behavior to another room, and then another, and so on until he is trained for the entire house. Going a step further, you must be watchful when visiting someone's home or a hotel, as house-training may not hold in a new location.

Initially limiting your puppy's freedom also makes supervision easier. Rather than chasing a fast, inquisitive puppy around the house to keep him from pottying where he shouldn't, you can watch him within his area while you perform every-day chores. Because most people choose a puppy area with a tile or linoleum floor for easy clean-up, the kitchen is a popular location. Having the puppy's area in the kitchen allows most owners to occupy themselves constructively while supervising puppy playtime.

SCHEDULE

Your puppy will typically need to potty right after eating, soon after drinking water, upon waking up from every nap, during or following playtime, and before bedtime. When the puppy is awake, he should be taken out about every hour until he is ten weeks old, after which point he can often wait a couple of hours and gradually increase from there. Even as an adult, however, your Aussie should not be asked to hold it for longer than five or six hours.

Keeping your puppy on a consistent schedule of eating, playing, pottying, and sleeping allows you to anticipate his calls to nature and therefore accomplish house-training more rapidly than you would with a casual or haphazard approach. Make sure that all family members adhere to the outlined schedule, or your puppy will experience "unexplained" house-training difficulties due to an erratic timetable.

As an example, leaving food available to your puppy all day may seem more convenient than scheduling three feedings a day, but it actually makes house-training far more difficult because you have no idea when your puppy will eat and thus no way to predict when he might need to go outside. This practice, called *free-feeding*, can also lead to the puppy's becoming overweight and subsequently

Did You Know? Puppies tend to potty in or near the same area all the time, gravitating to the odor left behind from previous eliminations. This explains why completely cleaning up and removing the odor after an indoor accident proves so important in preventing repeat trips to that spot.

When you take your puppy outside to potty, don't let him get distracted. Let him know that he must take care of business before he can play and explore.

House-training happens much faster when you keep your puppy on a set schedule even if your personal schedule varies. As house-training progresses, your puppy will try to wait until his usual outside trips to potty, but schedule irregularities make this control far more difficult for him to achieve.

suffering joint or other health problems. Only water should remain constantly available during your pup's active daytime hours to ensure proper hydration.

Dogs have an enviable internal clock—as anyone who has run late in feeding his or her adult dog quickly learns—and you can use it to your advantage in house-training. Maintaining a schedule helps your puppy learn when he will be let outside and thus to hold it until those times. As with feeding times, if you run late on letting your puppy out to potty, he will often whine to alert you to his discomfort, but he can only hold it for so long before the urge overtakes him.

When you enforce a consistent schedule, along with limited freedom, supervision, and crate confinement, your puppy should become rather reliably house-trained by the time he is four to five months old, and he should be trustworthy around the house by ten to twelve months of age. Your Aussie wants to please you and tries his best; he just needs your guidance in learning the rules and needs you to stick to the rules, too.

Once trained, your Australian Shepherd pup will know exactly where to go when it's potty time.

A common house-training mistake is allowing a young puppy run of the house. This is a vast environment from the puppy's point of view, an open invitation to have accidents. Puppies have no inhibition about eliminating where they play.
—Susan Meluzin, a professional dog handler and trainer in Flushing, New York

THE CRATE

For your Aussie, nothing compares to the joy of spending time with you and the family; however, this doesn't mean that he doesn't appreciate a little quiet time. A wire or plastic crate fits this purpose perfectly, providing a welcome retreat if your dog is introduced to it properly. Outfitted with a comfy bed and a variety of safe chew toys, your Aussie's crate not only provides him with his own private refuge but it also gives you a secure confinement area for those times when you cannot supervise your curious puppy.

People unfamiliar with crates often think it cruel to confine a dog in such a relatively small space, but this proves true only when owners use a too-small crate, overdo

Did You Know? Besides providing a refuge for your puppy when you cannot watch him, a crate helps the puppy gain control over his excretory system because puppies don't like to lie in puddles or messes. This also tells you that if your puppy has accidents in his crate, he needs more frequent trips outside or better supervision when outside to ensure that he actually goes.

confinement time, or keep the crate in a dark, damp, or isolated location. Dogs are natural den animals, meaning that in the wild they would seek out small caves or dig earthen dens where they could sleep and raise their young with protection from the weather.

Place your Aussie's crate in an out-of-the-way corner of a fairly busy room to give your puppy the security of knowing that his people are nearby. Feed him meals, offer him treats, and give him chew toys in the crate. Throw a treat or toy inside to encourage him to go into the crate. Show him that nice things happen in the crate, and soon he'll go in of his own accord for the occasional nap. Taking the time to build your pup's positive attitude toward the crate makes those inevitable longer confinements far more agreeable to your Australian Shepherd.

Teach your puppy a crate cue. Say "Crate" and toss a treat into the crate so that he enters the crate willingly. When letting him out, teach him to wait as you open the door. Find a quiet moment, toss in a treat to distract him, open the crate door, and gently but firmly put your hand on his chest as you say "Wait" and release him after a couple of seconds. Gradually build up the time. If he starts to rush out as you open the door, say "Uh-uh" and use the door to stop his forward motion.

CLEANING UP

There will be times when you miss your puppy's potty signals or you don't watch closely enough, and he'll have an accident indoors. After your verbal reminder ("No" or "Uh-uh") and a trip outdoors to let him finish, be sure to clean the spot thoroughly; a lingering odor can fool your puppy into thinking that it's an acceptable potty spot.

For slick flooring, cleaning up with paper towels and a quality pet-odor remover should suffice. For urine on carpet, immediately place paper towels or newspapers on top of the wet spot and apply pressure to increase absorption. Repeat until the towels come up fairly dry. Because hot water or steam cleaners set odors and urine stains, rinse the area with cool water, towel again, and follow with stain and odor remover. Leave several paper towels on top of the area for a couple hours to help absorb remaining urine; repeat the process until no urine odor remains. For solid waste, simply remove it and clean the area with an odor remover.

Your house-training efforts will pay off in a reliable Aussie who's a joy to live with.

Finding a trusted veterinarian to help care for your Aussie may be as easy as going to the same vet you've used with previous dogs or pets. First-time owners, however, will have some research to do. To avoid last-minute searching, do your investigation before you bring your puppy home. New owners should ask friends and neighbors about their vets and with whom they've had good and bad experiences. If a particular veterinarian gets glowing recommendations, it's worth meeting that person and finding out if he or she is taking on new clients.

If you meet a recommended vet and don't agree with your friends' opinions, try another veterinarian. The skilled vet who doesn't like or isn't knowledgeable about Aussies or who seems too rushed to answer your questions is not someone you really want to deal with repeatedly over the next twelve or so years. Additional

Though not common, allergic reactions to vaccines can occur within minutes or a few hours after injection. Signs include but aren't limited to vomiting, diarrhea, swelling, sudden itching, and labored breathing. If your puppy or dog exhibits any of these symptoms after a vaccination, call your veterinarian or an emergency clinic immediately.

it's a
Fact

factors, such as fees, office location, availability, and more, will enter into your decision-making process. A good long-term relationship with the right vet is well worth doing a little research beforehand. Here are some things to consider:

Attitude: Hopefully you'll only need to see your veterinarian at your Aussie's routine check-ups, but injuries and illnesses sometimes occur despite the best care. Regardless of the amount of medical attention your dog will need, you want a veterinarian who handles your Aussie with a confident manner, gentle respect, and an obvious affection for animals. He or she should be willing to answer your questions and, in the case of an illness or situation beyond his expertise, should refer you to a specialist who can care for your dog.

Costs: Veterinary costs are on the rise, and fees for routine procedures such as examinations and vaccinations vary among practices. For more advanced procedures, fees often depend on the individual practice's on-site medical equipment. The cost of such equipment naturally passes down to clients, but it also benefits clients by providing ready access to tests that might otherwise be more expensive or located farther away at a specialist's clinic or veterinary college.

Location: The mention of distance brings up the veterinarian's proximity to your home. Going to a nearby veterinarian obviously makes getting there easier,

and it also provides a sense of security to know that you can drive to your vet's office quickly in the event of a sudden injury or illness. Keep in mind, though, that many veterinary practices no longer offer after-hours emergency care. Discuss emergency services with any potential veterinarian. If the practice you choose does not offer after-hours care, you'll need to find out the location of the nearest emergency veterinary hospital.

Hours: When your work hours coincide with your veterinarian's office hours, you may find yourself scrambling to find another family member to take the dog in for appointments, or you may have to take time off of work. If this will present problems, you're better off to find a practice with evening or early morning hours that work with your own. Find out if the practice is open on weekends, if the vet has any emergency hours, and what the clinic's policies are for appointments and walk-in visits.

Rotation schedule: A veterinary practice often has three or four veterinarians on a rotating schedule within the office to cover appointment times more efficiently without any one doctor working too many hours. This also allows the veterinarians to consult with each other when needed and increases your chances of being "squeezed in" should something arise unexpectedly, because another vet can cover for his or her colleague.

Puppy owners must be careful in the waiting room of the veterinarian's office. Other well-intentioned owners often say that their dogs are friendly without really knowing if that friendliness extends to puppies. If you allow your Aussie to say hello, the result could be an unpleasant experience that will negatively affect [his] attitude toward other dogs and the veterinarian's office.

—Astrid Pryor, a trainer and rescue coordinator from Grass Valley, California

The downside to the rotation-type practice is that you don't always see the same veterinarian, and you may not feel comfortable with every vet in the practice. Though many offices allow you to request a specific veterinarian, if that vet has no appointments available when you want one, you may be asked to see a different doctor.

A one-veterinarian office gives you a better chance to know the person treating your dog, and gives the vet more of an opportunity to learn about your particular dog's personality and health, making for a nice symbiotic relationship. The downside here comes when your vet is completely booked or takes time off and has no alternate doctors on staff for you to see should your dog need attention. Most have on-call vets to cover for them or will at least refer clients to an emergency veterinary service when they cannot be on duty.

Cleanliness: Before you become a client, visit the veterinarian's office. It should be clean and free of offensive odors, short of a dog in the waiting room having an accident while you're there. The waiting room should look neat and orderly,

Did You Know?

Paw-pad injuries happen frequently and bleed profusely. Flush a mild cut with saline water to clean it and remove any debris, then apply light pressure with clean gauze to stop the bleeding. Wrapping the injury may be required to keep it clean enough to avoid infection, so your veterinarian might need to see your dog for bandaging.

as should the staff, who should greet you quickly and politely. Take this first overall impression very seriously because it tells you a lot about the veterinarian's attention to detail and hygiene.

YOUR FIRST APPOINTMENT

Once you find a veterinary facility that meets your needs, and if you plan to bring your puppy home soon or already have him home, make an appointment for a thorough check-over. If you bought your puppy from a reputable breeder, the breeder will insist that you have this veterinary examination done within a few days of purchase, as it ensures that the breeder sold you a healthy puppy. Your sales agreement from a good breeder likely includes a provision for a refund or a replacement puppy if a serious health problem turns up at this first veterinary appointment, as long as you take the puppy for an exam within the specified time frame. No matter, every new puppy should undergo an exam to rule out worms or other parasites as well as to schedule any vaccinations that he may require.

Buy a fun doggy toy to take along on your first vet visit. On appointment day, do not feed your puppy within about three hours of leaving to help prevent him from getting carsick or sick from anxiety or excitement. Arrive a few minutes early and ask the staff to give the toy to the veterinarian to win your puppy over. Avoid giving him treats at the vet's office, as treats could make him carsick on the way home. Your time in the waiting room gives your puppy a little time to look around, meet some of the staff, and take in the strange smells.

Before your puppy's vaccinations are complete, safeguard your puppy against contracting some nasty bug deposited on the floor or grounds by another dog by

Select a veterinarian with whom you and your Aussie are comfortable.

Just like infants, puppies need a series of vaccinations to ensure that they stay healthy during their first year of life. Download a vaccination chart from **DogChannel.com/Club-Aussie** that you can fill out for your Australian Shepherd.

carrying him rather than letting him walk around during his first veterinary visit. Absolutely keep your puppy away from other dogs, as you have no idea what could be ailing those fellow patients or how they will act toward your puppy, no matter what their owners say.

During this initial exam, in addition to giving your pup a parasite check and vaccines if needed, your vet will look for signs of anomalies such as eye disease, joint problems, heart trouble, and other ailments. The veterinarian may comment on your puppy's structure and how your puppy should develop. A well-bred Aussie should be structurally sound and built for athletic pursuits and endurance.

ABOUT VACCINATIONS

Simply put, vaccinations consist of killed or modified live viruses injected into or given intranasally to your dog to stimulate his body to produce protective antibodies against those diseases. Core vaccines, those recommended for all healthy puppies and dogs, include distemper, parvovirus, hepatitis, and rabies. The *Bordetella*, or kennel cough, vaccine might be required if your dog attends training classes or doggy day care, or may be recommended if you often visit dog parks or other places with many dogs, but immunity purportedly lasts for only a few months.

Your veterinarian might advise you to have your pup vaccinated against other diseases—such as leptospirosis, coronavirus, and canine parainfluenza—if they are prevalent in your area. The possibility of a vaccine reaction always exists, so do not take administering vaccinations too lightly. Debates currently rage over suspected links between vaccines and long-term immune-related diseases, such as allergies, cancer,

and others. Do some research and discuss benefits versus risks concerning the various vaccines with your veterinarian.

To help ensure that the vaccines will be effective, your puppy will undergo a series of three to four injections, depending on your veterinarian's preference, usually starting at eight to ten weeks of age and ending at roughly sixteen weeks of age. Though getting your puppy outside and around other dogs before finishing this series carries some risk, you'll miss an important window of opportunity if you wait until your puppy is four months old to begin socializing him. For this reason, many puppy kindergarten classes now accept puppies after their second round of shots.

Once your puppy completes his vaccinations, including the rabies vaccine, which is given in one injection and is the last vaccine given, the suggested frequency of vaccinations thereafter varies greatly among veterinarians, with some recommending yearly vaccines for maximum safety and others preferring a more conservative three-year schedule to lessen the chance of side effects. Again, personal research and a serious discussion with your vet will lead you to the decision that you feel best safeguards your Aussie's health.

FIRST-AID KIT

Accidents inevitably happen, and you should be prepared in advance. Having a doggy first-aid kit readily available in both your home and vehicle allows you to treat simple injuries yourself or gives you important extra time to get your dog to a veterinarian if needed. For easy access to important numbers in a hurry, put the phone numbers of your veterinarian, an emergency clinic, and a poison-control hotline on top of the kits. In case of a car accident, also include your name, phone number, and an emergency contact name and phone number in the car kit.

Among the items that should be included in your dog's first-aid kit are gauze, tweezers, antibiotic cream, antiseptic wipes, and blunt-ended scissors. You can purchase one of the many preassembled kits sold at pet-supply stores or talk to your veterinarian about how to make your own. Also consider purchasing a book on canine first-aid that details how to administer life-saving techniques like CPR, the Heimlich maneuver, and other emergency procedures.

COMMON PROBLEMS

Ah-choo: The viruses that cause human colds do not infect our dogs, but dogs can get runny noses, goopy eyes, and coughs for various reasons. For example, kennel cough is an often-vaccinated-against but still common virus that closely resembles the human cold and is noted for the continuous hacking cough it produces, mainly at night. Allergies, respiratory infections, and even heart conditions can also cause coughing, so your dog should see the vet if he experiences repeated coughing spells.

With all the sniffing he does, your Australian Shepherd might inhale some type of irritant and get a runny nose. This will pass once his nasal passages clear out the irritating substance, but a constant or frequent runny nose, possibly accompanied by sneezing, often denotes an allergy. Your veterinarian may recommend an antihistamine to relieve symptoms and make your dog more comfortable during prime allergy seasons. Prolonged severe sneezing can indicate the presence of a foreign body lodged in your dog's sinuses, requiring a trip to the vet to have it removed.

Ouch: Deep cuts of any size require immediate professional attention, but your active Aussie will no doubt sustain a few minor cuts or scrapes that warrant care but not necessarily a trip to the vet. To clean a cut, flush it with warm water or a saline solution, making sure to remove any debris, and then apply an antibiotic cream for dogs to the wound. Check the cut frequently to ensure that it's healing well and not becoming infected.

Tummy troubles: Somewhat of a scavenger by nature, your Aussie will occasionally eat something in the yard or on a walk that doesn't agree with his tummy. Overfeeding, giving too many rich snacks, leaving the garbage within reach, and other owner mistakes also contribute to stomach or intestinal upsets in dogs. Stress can produce the same unfortunate upsets; in this case, troubles occur in situations that make the dog feel anxious, such as

NOTABLE & QUOTABLE

Overheating is a life-threatening emergency. Many dogs don't slow down when reaching the point at which they should stop exercising, so it's important for you to know when enough is enough. If you fear that your dog is overheating, wet his stomach and paw pads with cool water and seek veterinary attention immediately. Never ice your dog, as this can make the effects worse!
—Nicole Kelly, an emergency veterinary technician from Tucson, Arizona

traveling or being left home alone for longer than usual.

If your dog experiences repeated episodes of severe vomiting, intense diarrhea for more than a few hours, or a combination thereof, take him to the veterinarian. He may have contracted a virus, picked up some type of bacteria, or be suffering from a dangerous blockage caused by swallowing something that you probably do not even know about. For minor vomiting or diarrhea, skip a meal to let his digestive system rest and then, at the next feeding, give him a small bland meal. Many veterinarians recommend cooked chicken and rice or a prescription canned food for a couple of days. If all seems well after that, you can reintroduce his regular food.

Smelly glands: All dogs have two sacs below the anus; these glands contain a strong, unpleasant-smelling liquid that is expressed in small amounts through openings beside the anus each time your dog defecates. Sometimes these glands become too full and uncomfortable, causing your dog to scoot his rear on the ground in an attempt to empty them. Licking around the anus also can indicate an anal-gland problem.

Dogs demonstrating discomfort with their anal glands probably need their glands manually expressed, an unpleasant but necessary task to prevent the glands from becoming impacted and possibly infected. Glands must be emptied correctly to avoid damage; this is something that your veterinarian can do. If your dog experiences ongoing problems that require gland expression every week or two, your vet can show you how to do it safely. You can also ask your groomer to do it if you have your Aussie groomed professionally, as most groomers know how to express the glands.

Heatstroke: The canine cooling system limits a dog's ability to withstand heat extremes in that a dog cools himself mainly by panting and sweating from the paw pads. This inefficient system can result in overheating, heat exhaustion, and heatstroke when the dog overdoes it in warmer temperatures, particularly above 80 degrees Fahrenheit. Energetic dogs like the Aussie don't always know when to quit, leaving it up to the observant owner to make sure that the dog rests before he shows signs of overheating, which include:

- excessive, rapid panting
- trembling
- stumbling
- glassy eyes
- vomiting
- diarrhea

Should symptoms occur, pour cool—not cold—water over your Australian Shepherd, especially on the belly, between the legs, and on the head. Turning on a fan or getting the dog into air conditioning also helps. Most veterinarians advise you to avoid icing your dog down, as icing will constrict the blood flow and can worsen the condition. As soon as your Aussie cools down, take him for a veterinary check-up to assure a full recovery.

Did You Know?

Many people think that if a dog is scooting his rear across the ground, it means that he has worms. That can be the case, but dogs often scoot their rears in response to full or impacted anal glands.

Panting is the normal way that dogs keep cool, but be on the lookout for any signs of overheating in your active Australian Shepherd.

CONCERNS

For the Australian Shepherd to enjoy life to the fullest, he needs a loving owner who does his or her best to ensure that this wonderful companion stays as healthy as possible. An Aussie owner must be aware of potential genetic problems in the breed and those that result from environment, diet, or contact with unhealthy dogs. Though the list of possible ailments is long, take heart in knowing that Aussies generally possess good health and longevity, and most of this knowledge will be simply for precautionary purposes.

JOINT PROBLEMS

Joint issues that can be seen in the Australian Shepherd are by no means unique to the breed. Of the three that follow, hip dysplasia is the most commonly seen in the Aussie. Awareness of these diseases starts with a reputable breeder, who does his or her best to use only sound breeding stock so that the Australian Shepherd will continue to be

Did You Know? Orthopedic specialists utilize numerous surgical treatments for canine hip dysplasia, including total hip joint replacement. Though hip replacement is a major procedure with numerous possible complications, the surgery's success rate for producing pain-free movement has been rated as high as more than 90 percent.

SMART TIP!

Because excess weight stresses growing joints, obesity in puppies is believed to be a contributing factor toward the development of orthopedic problems. Keep your Aussie puppy at an ideal weight per your veterinarian's recommendations to help his joints stay healthy as he matures.

the physically fit breed that it is meant to be—capable of strenuous work and athletic endeavors.

Hip Dysplasia

Ranging from a mildly uncomfortable to a sometimes debilitating malformation of the canine hip joint, hip dysplasia can occur in any breed. Various studies show a strong genetic factor in the development of this orthopedic disorder, a fact that underlines the importance of buying an Australian Shepherd puppy from parents whose hips have been verified as healthy through x-ray examination by qualified specialists.

Two major organizations certify hip-joint health: the Orthopedic Foundation for Animals (OFA) and the University of Pennsylvania School of Veterinary Medicine, whose hip-screening program is known as PennHip. The OFA test evaluates a dog's radiographs to determine how well the leg's femoral head fits into the hip-joint socket, and each dog is issued a hip rating. Dogs rated Excellent, Good, and Fair are issued OFA numbers, while dogs rated Borderline or with dysplasia of any degree (categorized as Mild, Moderate, and Severe) do not qualify for OFA numbers. PennHip's screening process takes a somewhat different approach: its veterinarians

evaluate x-rays to determine the presence of hip dysplasia by measuring hip laxity and looking for signs of osteoarthritis.

Besides genetics, factors such as diet, weight, and exercise are believed to affect joint health. An ill-balanced diet or improper supplementation, resulting in too-rapid growth, can intensify dysplasia, and many veterinarians warn that excess weight on a young puppy presents another possible contributing factor. A puppy who comes from certified non-dysplastic parents, who is fed a quality diet, and who is allowed free exercise through normal play and exploration stands the best chance for healthy hips as an adult.

One of the puzzles associated with this disorder relates to the symptoms shown by affected puppies and dogs. One dog may demonstrate difficulty getting up, odd movement when walking or running, stiffness, and limping, while another dog may show none of these signs even if more severely afflicted. As arthritis inevitably develops in the malformed joints, symptoms often become more apparent or severe. Any suspicion that your Aussie may suffer from hip dysplasia warrants a veterinary examination.

A diagnosis of hip dysplasia does not mean that your Aussie's life is over. Treatment options run the gamut from natural supplements to pain relievers to surgical procedures, and the best choice depends on the individual dog and the severity of his condition. Properly treated hip dysplasia may not even slow down your active Australian Shepherd.

Elbow Dysplasia

Elbow dysplasia resembles hip dysplasia in that it is a malformation of the joint, this time that of the elbow. Discomfort, pain,

NOTABLE & QUOTABLE

*Many serious health issues can't be tested for, includ-
ing epilepsy, autoimmune [diseases], and early cancers.
Breeding too young compounds the risks. For instance, the
average age of onset of seizures is two to four years. If a dog
is good at two years old, he or she will be a much better breeding choice at four,
when the greatest chance of developing a disease has passed.*
—Janet Hanson, owner of Crystal Canyon Australian Shepherds in Trail, Oregon

Stoic by nature, dogs don't readily show illness or pain. Note how your Aussie acts on a daily basis and watch for anything "out-of-sorts," such as decreased interest in play, changes in potty habits, a slight limp, excessive scratching at an ear—anything that might tell you that he needs your help to feel better.

swelling, and eventual arthritis accompany this condition, with varying degrees of lameness frequently present in the affected foreleg. As with hip dysplasia, genetics play a large role in the development of this disorder, so look for a puppy whose parents' elbows have been certified as normal by the OFA.

The success of surgical treatments varies, with most owners opting to manage the condition with pain medications, natural supplements, and weight control. Suitable exercise to build the surrounding muscles without overtaxing the joint proves very helpful. Low-impact activities like on-leash walks or tracking provide superior exercise for dogs suffering from joint problems, but swimming offers the most beneficial, least jarring exercise possible, and it's something that most dogs love when introduced to water slowly and encouragingly.

Osteochondritis Dissecans (OCD)

Not a widespread disease in the Australian Shepherd but one of which Aussie owners should be aware, OCD originates in the immature dog by affecting the cartilage in various joints. Particularly common in the shoulder, OCD creates internal irritation due to a "flap" in improperly formed cartilage. This irritation causes pain and subsequent constant or intermittent limping. Genetic predisposition, trauma, rapid growth, and other factors are suspected contributors. Pain relievers in mild cases and surgical removal of the irritating cartilage in more severe cases remain the usual treatments.

EYE PROBLEMS

Eye problems are not uncommon in the Aussie, and reputable breeders have their dogs' eyes examined by board-certified veterinary ophthalmologists for certification with the Canine Eye Registration Foundation (CERF). CERF maintains a canine eye-health database by recording test results and issuing certification to dogs with normal test results. Yearly eye testing is recommended, especially for Aussies used in breeding programs, as some eye problems do not present themselves until later in life.

Cataracts

Cataracts can result from old age, injury, or as side effects of another disease, but the most common form of cataracts is hereditary. Because hereditary cataracts may not show up until a dog reaches his senior years and no known genetic marker exists, eliminating this disease proves difficult. Starting as a smallish blur, a cataract progresses in size until it is visible as an opaque cloud on the eye that eventually can cause blindness.

Surgical removal of the cataract has been the most successful treatment method thus far, but some owners opt for an experimental noninvasive treatment using eye drops intended to dissolve the cataract over time. The latter's effectiveness seems to be under debate, but it is hoped that it will prove successful.

Iris Coloboma

In this eye affliction that can be found in the Australian Shepherd, part of the dog's iris is missing, and the remaining iris is unable to contract to block out bright light; thus, affected dogs are light sensitive. Though undoubtedly making an affected dog uncomfortable on sunny days, this condition, usually present from birth, causes no apparent pain. No treatment exists, and it is recommended that an affected dog wear doggy sunglasses. Your veterinarian or a CERF examination should detect iris coloboma if present.

Collie Eye Anomaly (CEA)

Named for the breed most commonly afflicted, CEA occasionally affects Australian Shepherds. The CEA designation really covers several congenital developmental defects. Most of these defects barely affect vision throughout the dog's life, but some more serious cases lead to eventual blindness. A veterinary ophthalmologist can detect the disease very early; examination and diagnosis is recommended before a puppy reaches eight weeks of age.

Affected dogs adapt to the slight loss of vision but should not be used for breeding to prevent the spread of this genetic disorder among the Aussie population. DNA testing can be performed to identify those dogs that are carriers of the gene mutation responsible for CEA. Generally, no treatment is recommended or even needed unless dealing with a severe case that may require surgical intervention to minimize vision loss or prevent blindness.

AUTOIMMUNE DISEASES

An autoimmune disease is one in which the body's defenses toward outside invaders turn inward and destroy essential tissues.

Autoimmune diseases are seen in all breeds of dogs and in mixed breeds as well. Two are explained here; generalized demodectic mange is another but is mentioned in the section on mites.

Autoimmune Thyroiditis or Hypothyroidism

In this case, the body's defenses attack the thyroid gland. As this occurs, generally one or more symptoms, such as hair loss, unexplained weight gain, thickened skin, and lethargy, become evident. Blood tests can reveal this problem but they do not always produce clear-cut results, calling for repeated tests in the future if symptoms persist. If your Australian Shepherd displays any of the aforementioned signs, take him in for bloodwork before his symptoms progress to the point of making him miserable.

A relatively inexpensive medication usually balances hormone levels to reduce or eliminate symptoms, though some dogs respond to treatment better than others do. Genetic ties have been established, and the OFA now records test results so that breeders can make informed decisions about which breeding lines are less likely to produce puppies predisposed to thyroid problems.

Lupus

Lupus occurs infrequently in dogs. This disease finds the body's defenses attacking various organs—the less severe form of the disease manifests itself in skin lesions, but it can advance to affect other organs, including the kidneys, heart, joints, and lungs. Skin lesions, lethargy, intermittent fever, shifting lameness, increased thirst and urination, and other symptoms are possible indicators of lupus.

Most veterinarians treat lupus with corticosteroids, but a dog with lupus must be monitored carefully to help prevent secondary infections. Some vets recommend vitamin E and other supplements to boost the immune system. Experts suspect but have not yet established a genetic factor.

ALLERGIES

Allergies emerge when the body's immune system overreacts to normal substances as if they pose a threat. Almost rampant these days, canine allergies run the gamut from flea to inhalant to contact to food. Though an allergic reaction can take the form of a runny nose and irritated eyes, dogs usually manifest allergies through symptoms such as welts, rashes, ear infections, itchy feet, and the like. Digestive troubles, such as vomiting and diarrhea, are also common, though they may indicate food intolerance rather than a true allergy unless accompanied by skin problems.

The intense itching produced by an allergic reaction causes the dog to scratch, chew, and lick affected areas to the point that they may become raw, hairless, and even bloody, making the dog and his concerned owner miserable. Some allergies, such as those to pollen or grasses, are seasonal, while others last all year long. Medicated, hydrocortisone, oatmeal, and other specialty shampoos can help alleviate symptoms, as can limiting or eliminating exposure to the allergen, if it is known. Finding the trigger in most cases requires either food trials or experimenting with the products used in the dog's environment; more severe cases will require allergy testing by a veterinary dermatologist. To improve skin condition and promote better general health, a diet upgrade is often necessary, even if the dog is not allergic to food. A multifaceted approach helps heal the allergy sufferer inside and out.

Flea Allergies

Sometimes determining the cause and solution of an allergy is as easy as finding a few fleas on your constantly scratching dog and eradicating them with one of the many flea-control products on the market. Flea removal must be complete, as just one flea can send a flea-allergic dog into a scratching and chewing frenzy. Ask your vet to recommend safe products to use on your Australian Shepherd and around your home to get rid of fleas, and also ask about safe flea preventives, some of which also repel ticks and other pests.

Inhalant and Contact Allergies

A dog with an allergy to pollen, grass, house dust, or something else beyond your control within his immediate environment makes avoiding the allergen source impossible. Add to this the outright bombardment of allergy triggers found in spring and summer, and the stage is set for severe reactions. Allergic reactions to pollen, grass, and the like typically begin in younger dogs and start out as seasonal flare-ups, but affected dogs eventually exhibit symptoms year-round. Dogs can also be allergic to substances in the home—such as the soap you use to wash his bedding, the carpeting in your living room, or the plastic in his food bowl, to name just a few—over which you have control. When the trigger can be identified and removed from the dog's environment, allergy symptoms often improve dramatically, but finding the culprit requires acute observation.

Veterinarians often prescribe corticosteroids or antihistamines to relieve allergy

Emergencies and health problems are often unforeseen. If your dog needs to be hospitalized, you want the experience to be as low-stress as possible so your dog can focus on feeling better [and is] not stressing about being caged. Dogs that have been properly crate-trained don't often exhibit the anxiety seen in untrained dogs when hospitalized.

—Nicole Kelly, an emergency veterinary technician from Tucson, Arizona

symptoms, generally in combination with specialty shampoos to soothe the skin. Sprays, supplements, and hyposensitization shots (immunotherapy) may be recommended.

Food Allergies

Food allergies tend to be as challenging to pinpoint as any other, with possible triggers including beef, chicken, soy, wheat, corn, and many more of the ingredients commonly found in dog foods. Switching to a prescription diet available through your veterinarian or a homemade diet that comprises ingredients not found in his regular food can help the allergy symptoms clear up. A gradual, one-at-a-time reintroduction to previous foods will single out which ones initiate problems.

INTERNAL PARASITES

Intestinal or other internal parasites, such as the various types of worms, are relatively common in the canine population. Puppies prove particularly susceptible to worms, as their immune systems are not fully developed, allowing nasty critters an easier takeover than in a healthy adult.

Senior dogs with weakened immune systems can also be at greater risk of developing worm populations if exposed.

Because dogs and even people can inadvertently pick up worm eggs shed in feces, always clean up doggy waste right away using plastic bags or a poop scooper to safeguard against the spread of worms and for general cleanliness. Though most healthy adult dogs' systems naturally resist worm infestation, all dogs should have yearly fecal checks performed by their veterinarians as a precaution or at any time a worm infestation is suspected. Many of the monthly heartworm preventives available today also protect our pets from other worms.

Heartworms

Passed on to a dog through the bite of a larvae-carrying mosquito, heartworms mature within the dog's pulmonary arteries, heart, and lungs. In mild infestations, the only apparent symptom might be a slight cough, whereas more advanced cases produce a marked cough, exercise intolerance, liver enlargement, and possible death. Heartworm infestation is a serious condition; fortunately, it does not affect humans.

Certainly prevention is the best medicine for heartworm, and your veterinarian can recommend and prescribe a safe heartworm preventive, usually taken monthly, for your Aussie. Yearly heartworm testing is done as an added precaution. Once heartworms take hold, treatment becomes expensive and risky, as it involves using a very strong drug to kill the worms. Once killed, the worms can still form blockages in the dog's blood vessels. With otherwise healthy dogs, treatment is usually successful.

Did You Know?

Dogs incur poisonous snake bites with some regularity, which is not surprising, considering that they love sticking their noses under logs, bushes, and rocks. In areas where rattlesnakes are prevalent, many owners have their dogs trained by professionals who use muzzled snakes and electric collars to teach rattlesnake avoidance.

Keeping your Aussie's out-door areas clean is a necessary preventive measure against parasites. You don't want your dog's roll in the grass to turn into something problematic.

Roundworms

The most common intestinal worms in dogs, roundworms appear as tan or whitish 2- to 4-inch long spaghetti-like strands when passed in a dog's stool or vomit. A perfectly healthy female can harbor dormant roundworm larvae that migrate to her puppies in the womb or through her milk after birth; thus, most breeders "worm" puppies with a veterinarian-prescribed wormer before sending them home.

A previously wormed puppy can pick up roundworms through the plentiful eggs lurking in his environment thanks to the parasite's various hosts. An infested animal suffers a poor coat, a bloated belly, an obviously itchy anus, and possibly vomiting and diarrhea. Frequent fecal checks during puppyhood can detect shed eggs so that the worms producing them can be eliminated before symptoms occur. Left unchecked, roundworms can produce an intestinal blockage or migrate to the lungs and potentially kill a puppy or unhealthy adult.

Hookworms

Unlike roundworms, which feed off predigested material passing through the digestive system, hookworms use tiny teeth to attach to the intestinal wall and drink the host's blood. Once these worms become established, it doesn't take long for them to cause what can become serious anemia, leaving the host weak and thin, with pale gums and dark-colored stools. In time, the blood loss can result in the dog's needing blood transfusions or can prove fatal, especially in young puppies or seniors.

Transmission to the host occurs much the same as it does in roundworms—either through the mom or the environment. Once detected, hookworms are treatable, but as always, preventive measures are best.

Cleanliness, regular canine fecal checks, and appropriate medications can stop this nasty worm from finding a home; many of the heartworm preventives also protect against hookworms. Hookworms can cause an easily treatable but uncomfortable skin condition in humans when bare skin comes in contact with larvae, but people do not incur intestinal infestation from the common canine hookworm.

Tapeworms

A dog most often develops a tapeworm infestation from ingesting the most common intermediate host—the bane of dogs everywhere—the flea. A dog that has fleas chews himself as the fleas bite and move around on his body, causing him to occasionally swallow some of these tapeworm carriers. A different type of tapeworm can occur if your dog eats a rabbit or mouse. Once ingested, the immature worms in the intermediate host attach to the dog's intestinal wall and absorb nutrients, enabling the worms to grow into thin, flat, segmented adults.

The egg-containing segments eventually detach and can often be seen as rice-like particles around the dog's anus or in the stool. Fortunately, tapeworms usually do little harm, but a serious infestation can result in general malaise. Dogs cannot transmit tapeworms directly to humans, but a person can be infested by swallowing a carrier flea. Obviously, flea control and not allowing your dog to eat small wild animals are necessary precautions. If tapeworms are detected, your veterinarian will provide a suitable wormer.

Whipworms

Whipworms produce hardy eggs that are able to withstand freezing temperatures and lie in wait in the soil, possibly for

Lethargy can indicate any number of problems, so watch for signs that your Australian Shepherd isn't feeling like his usual energetic self.

years, until an unsuspecting canine eats or drinks from a contaminated source or inadvertently ingests some eggs while nosing about. Once internal, the young worms hatch and attach to the dog's intestinal wall, where they feed on blood and tissue secretions. The dog is usually asymptomatic unless infestation becomes heavy, in which case mucus-thick chronic diarrhea can occur.

Because eggs don't pass with every stool, veterinarians find fecal checks to be unreliable in diagnosing whipworms, and they may prescribe wormers to dogs who show symptoms as a safety measure. Though worming medications kill established worms, the shed eggs' ability to withstand harsh conditions causes dogs to become infested again, often over and over. Covering infected soil with a fresh layer of dirt, gravel, or concrete sometimes proves

the only way to avert repeated exposure. Whipworms do not affect humans.

Giardia and Coccidia

These are not worms, but are parasitic protozoa that enter your dog as he eats or drinks from an area contaminated with cysts shed through infected animals' feces. The parasites then inhabit the dog's intestines and eventually can interfere with digestion to the point that they cause diarrhea, which can range from mild to severe. Puppies and adult dogs with compromised immune systems are particularly susceptible to serious infestation.

Various drugs effectively eliminate these parasitic invaders from your puppy's or dog's intestines. Picking up after your dog and disinfecting the areas that he frequents should kill them off in the environment, and keeping the dog's coat clean will ensure that the coat stays free of fecal matter. Prevent an infestation by not allowing your dog to drink from puddles, streams, lakes, and the like. *Giardia* can potentially cross over to humans, but *coccidia* infection in dogs does not affect humans.

EXTERNAL PARASITES

Long the curse of canines everywhere, pests such as fleas, ticks, and mites can cause itchy, painful skin conditions and more serious diseases.

Fleas

These blood-sucking parasites live on your dog and in his environment. In fact, it is estimated that only about 5 percent of the actual flea population resides on your dog, and the rest consists of eggs and larvae that live outdoors in milder temperatures and indoors year-round in the comfortable ambient temperatures that we humans prefer, giving mature fleas easy access to your dog and family. Though fleas prefer dogs, humans suffice in a pinch.

Flea saliva is an extremely irritating substance, intensifying the itching already caused by the parasites crawling around on the body and biting the skin. Many dogs exhibit allergic reactions to flea bites, causing them to frantically scratch and chew at themselves, making the skin raw. And, as mentioned, fleas can also transmit tapeworm because they act as one of the worm's intermediary hosts.

Chances are, if you find fleas on your dog, they also inhabit your house. Many people swear that their house is flea-free

Your Aussie's abundant coat and love of the outdoors make him a target for pests that can cause itching or worse.

until they go on vacation and return to a plethora of hungry pests. Ridding the dog and the environment of fleas requires killing fleas at all life stages until none are left to reproduce.

A combination of natural products and chemicals is generally the safest and most effective means of eliminating fleas. For instance, fleas can drown, so a daily bath in a mild dog shampoo will kill many fleas if you wet and soap your dog well, let him soak for a few minutes, rinse like crazy, and repeat. Once the flea population on your dog is reduced, a more permanent flea-control product, such as a monthly topical preventive as recommended by your vet, can be used. Frequently washing your dog's bedding or favorite napping rugs, which are common drop-off points for fleas and eggs, further reduces their numbers.

Spraying the house with a chemical designed to kill developing fleas usually works to rid your home of these pests. A piece of a strong flea collar placed into your vacuum bag—an otherwise perfect feeding ground for young fleas—will prevent them from making this a temporary home. Countless chemical and natural products can help you liberate yourself, your home, and your dog from these parasites, but doing so requires a broad attack and dedication to the cause. With today's advances in flea control, there's no reason for your dog to suffer these nasty parasites.

Ticks

Blood-sucking ticks carry a number of diseases that can be transmitted to dogs after they attach and feed, with Lyme disease and Rocky Mountain spotted fever two of the best known and most prevalent. Ticks detect potential hosts through heat signatures as they lurk along hiking trails, near wooded paths, and in grasses and vegetation, waiting for animals or people to pass. When a tick detects a promising host, it merely grabs hold of or drops onto its victim and crawls to an area unimpeded by too much hair or fur, which explains why you often find ticks on a dog's ears or face.

As with fleas, there are numerous products that repel or kill ticks. Spring generally finds ticks at their most abundant, as anyone who has ever walked his or her dog in a wooded area in April or May can attest. In certain areas, without a tick repellent, you could find ten to twenty ticks on your dog or yourself afterward. Avoiding heavy vegetation during the height of tick season, keeping your lawn short to prevent ticks from settling in, and checking your dog frequently for unwanted passengers provide added protection.

Mites

Mites can cause problems in dogs and result in what is commonly referred to as *mange*. Types of mange include demodectic, sarcoptic, and otodectic, with the variety of mange depending on the variety of mite that infests your dog. These microscopic beings can wreak havoc on the dog's coat, skin, and ears. Puppies and dogs with compromised immune systems

Just one flea on a dog with a flea allergy can send him into a skin- and coat-chewing frenzy that leaves the area red, raw, and furless, possibly leading to a skin infection called a *hot spot* that may require veterinary attention.

it's a Fact

generally suffer the worst cases of mange and require careful treatment and management in some cases to recover fully.

Demodectic mange: The *Demodex* mite is normally present in small numbers on your dog's skin. Overpopulation can occur in a puppy, due to the youngster's immature immune system, or in an adult dog with immune-system problems. Local demodectic mange results in small patches of hair loss around the facial area that often clear up when the animal's immune system begins to function properly, whereas the generalized variety spreads over the dog's entire body and usually requires medical intervention to prevent secondary infections. Demodectic mange is not contagious.

Sarcoptic mange: Also known as *scabies*, this highly contagious condition causes severe itching and resultant scratching that work together to produce hair loss, lesions, crusty skin, and other effects. This type of mange usually forms on the face, elbows, or belly first, manifesting in red welt-like patches that gradually spread over the entire body if left untreated. Because these mites can pass to humans, owners should follow their veterinarian's recommendations about handling the affected dog, and the dog should not have contact with other dogs until cured. Several treatments exist for sarcoptic mange; with diligent care and handling, the prognosis for recovery is good in reasonably healthy animals.

Otodectic mange: Ear mites also find puppies and dogs with weakened immune systems to be the easiest targets. These mites transfer readily from dog to dog, which explains the usual mode of infestation, and can lead to otodectic mange. This mange usually, but not always, is limited to the area around the outer ear canal, and it causes the dog to shake his head and scratch at his itchy ears. The red, crusty, scabby mess that results requires dedicated treatment to eliminate. Ear mites do not transfer to humans but can easily affect other pets in the household, who will then also require treatment.

SEIZURES

Idiopathic epileptic seizures, meaning those of unknown causes, unfortunately occur with some regularity in the Australian Shepherd. A seizure happens in response to what might be described as a neurologic outburst in the brain with symptoms that may start as a body tremor and often progress to muscle convulsions, clenching of the teeth, salivation, glazed eyes, and unresponsiveness to you or the environment. Seizures usually last anywhere from less than a minute to five minutes, and they end with an upset, confused, and frightened dog.

Cluster seizures also occur in the Australian Shepherd. This means that the dog suffers a stream of continuous seizures that present a very serious situation for the owner, who must get the dog to the veterinarian as soon as possible in hopes of preventing permanent damage. These types of seizures can result from toxins, head injuries, low blood sugar, or other problems, but most are believed to be hereditary, and scientists currently seek genetic markers that could help breeders eliminate this devastating problem from the gene pool. Anyone who has witnessed his or her Aussie experiencing a seizure appreciates the urgent need to beat this condition.

Should your dog be unfortunate enough to suffer a seizure, keep your hand away from his mouth in case his teeth clench uncontrollably. However, dogs do not swallow their tongues. Try to keep your dog from hurting himself during convulsions by gently scooting his body away from hard objects and putting something soft under his head. Remain calm and pay attention to what your dog does during and after a seizure, as well as how long the seizure lasts, so you can record this data later for the veterinarian.

Your veterinarian will perform bloodwork and a thorough examination to look for physical causes of the seizures. Sometimes correcting another problem will stop the seizures. If nothing is found and the seizures continue, medication and possibly holistic supplements may be prescribed to help reduce the number and severity of the seizures, thus making both the dog and the caring owner more comfortable while reducing the chances of brain damage or possible death.

CANCER

Assorted cancers affect dogs of all breeds and ages and are a leading cause of death among canines. Lymphoma, osteosarcoma, various organ cancers, and many others affect our dogs. You may notice symptoms such as lumps, bumps, limping, changes in potty habits, and weight loss, depending on the attacking cancer. As in humans, catching cancer in its early stages greatly increases the chance of the dog's overcoming the disease, but the stoic nature of most dogs often makes it difficult for owners to know that something is wrong until it is too late.

Check your Australian Shepherd frequently for suspicious growths, swelling, inflamed areas, or any other abnormalities that you can see or feel, and note any changes in his potty habits, appetite,

thirst, and energy level—basically, look for any indicators that something might be wrong. Radiographs, ultrasounds, and biopsies are among the tests that might be recommended. Most of the time, everything turns out fine, but when cancer is diagnosed, treatment could include surgery, drugs, specialized diets, chemotherapy, and natural supplements to boost digestion and overall health. With proper treatment, many dogs recover completely or at least enjoy quality of life for their remaining time.

Your Aussie is a hardy dog who can withstand rough terrain and weather, but he still depends on you to look out for his health.

What you feed your Australian Shepherd will be reflected in his coat, skin, eyes, and overall health, which makes the choice of diet one of the most important decisions you'll make in caring for your Aussie. Feed him poorly, and his coat will be lackluster, his skin either greasy or dry, and his eyes dull. Feed him well, and his coat will gleam with that lovely Aussie sheen and bright coloring, his skin will glow with health, and his eyes will glisten brilliantly.

In addition to looking good, your Aussie will feel better, work better, and play better when you provide the nutrition that this energetic breed needs. Countless brands and types of dog food line the shelves of pet-supply stores, offering a wide but rather confusing assortment, with each package declaring that what's inside is the best food for your pet. Despite these claims, quality in dog foods varies, just as it does

Consistently withholding water from your puppy or dog to reduce the number of times that he needs to go out to relieve himself can result in **dehydration** and too-concentrated urine that opens the door to bacterial infections. Ample water hydrates and flushes the kidneys, bladder, and urinary tract to help keep these organs healthy.

it's a Fact

Keep dry and canned dog foods in a cool, dry location to prevent heat and humidity from turning the fats rancid. Store opened dry food in the bag inside an airtight, food-approved container for no more than thirty days. Cover and refrigerate open cans and use the food within three days. Never use any food past the manufacturer's expiration date.

in any type of product, so learning about the different types of foods and what your Aussie requires should help you sort things out and make the right decisions.

DIET TYPES

Dry dog food, or kibble, by far represents the most popular type of dog food available. Conveniently packaged, easy to feed, and well liked by most dogs, kibble comes in large-bite, small-bite, puppy-growth, adult-maintenance, and senior-wellness formulas—and many more. Because the majority of moisture is removed in processing, kibble provides condensed nutrition relative to the amount fed, which makes it more cost-effective than foods with high moisture content. Dry foods do require chemical or natural preservatives to maintain their freshness.

Wet food can contain around 70 percent moisture and comes in cans or sometimes pouches. Because processing wet food is less involved than processing kibble, wet food retains more of the ingredients' flavor and texture, which usually means that dogs like it better than kibble. The downside comes from the higher cost and the fact that the elevated moisture content creates a less dense food. Your dog will need to eat more canned food than kibble to get the nutrition that he needs. To offset the cost but still offer their dogs the enjoyment of canned food, many owners combine wet food with kibble.

Semi-moist foods are often made to resemble meat, such as hamburger, but they contain ingredients that are as unhealthy for our dogs as they are for us. Dogs find this food appealing because most dogs like sweets, and these foods generally contain a considerable amount of sugar, corn syrup, or another type of sweetener in addition to salt, chemical dyes, and chemical preservatives. While perhaps fine as an occasional treat, these foods are not a healthy component of your dog's main diet.

Frozen dog foods have come to the forefront in recent years, offering a fresher nutritional source than processed diets. Many companies provide frozen raw-food diets consisting of meat, vegetables, fruit, and other ingredients in varying percentages. Not everyone feels that frozen raw diets—even those produced by well-known companies—are safe from pathogenic contamination, but this market segment continues to grow despite the relatively high cost and lesser convenience.

Dehydrated and freeze-dried pet foods are gaining in popularity. Most dogs find these foods palatable after rehydration, and both purportedly retain many of the ingredients' natural benefits. Almost as convenient as kibble, these diets especially bear consideration for dogs not faring well on kibble or other foods.

NUTRITION BASICS

You and your Australian Shepherd have similar basic nutritional needs but in different proportions due to the canine's

Believe it or not, during your Aussie's lifetime, you'll buy a few hundred pounds of dog food! Go to **DogChannel.com/Club-Aussie** and download a chart that outlines the cost of dog food.

High-quality dog foods cost more initially but provide superior digestibility and more concentrated nutrients, meaning that your Aussie will require less food to obtain proper nutrition and maintain his ideal weight. This combination makes for a long-term cost-effective purchase that helps keep your dog healthy and trim.

carnivorous origins. For instance, whereas doctors often advise humans to eat more fruits and vegetables with less meat, dogs do best with a diet high in meat protein. This shouldn't be surprising when you consider the large ruminants and small mammals that make up the bulk of a wild dog's diet and that the domesticated dog's digestive system essentially replicates that of its feral cousins.

Ample protein from appropriate sources aids in growth, muscle development, organ performance, and every other bodily function. Because the canine does not possess the proper dental structure or digestive system to adequately break down the protein from grain sources, corn and other grains should not comprise the main protein source in your dog's food. Chicken, beef, lamb, and turkey are popular protein bases found in premium-quality dog foods, providing your dog a digestible form of this vital nutrient.

Because dogs fare better on meat protein, some controversy surrounds the ample use of carbohydrates in dog food. Particularly abundant in dry dog foods, carbohydrates do provide a readily accessible and less expensive food source that helps dogs feel full and keep costs down. The principal purpose behind carbohydrates is for the body to convert the sugars and starches into energy and utilize the fiber as a digestive aid.

Crucial for skin and coat health; hormone production; utilization of vitamins A, D, and E; and many other bodily activities, fats also serve as an energy source. Though dogs produce some fatty acids on their own, essential fatty acids must be supplied in the diet through ingredients such as chicken fat, salmon oil, or sunflower oil. Because fats will go rancid and make your dog ill unless preserved in some manner, manufacturers use preservatives or processing methods to maintain their freshness.

The various vitamins and minerals present in fresh foods—or added back into processed foods—play a role in every bodily function, including growth, muscle condition, nerve stability, and immune-system health. These nutrients must be provided in correct amounts, as too little or too much

Don't forget to bring along food and water when you and your Aussie are on the go.

can wreak havoc on the organs, skeletal structure, nervous system, and so on. Oversupplementation has become a problem among owners who want to ensure that their dogs receive all of the nutrients they need but forget that there can be too much of a good thing.

Perhaps the most vital nutrient that your Aussie needs is water. Without adequate water, his body will not function properly, even if he eats the highest quality diet. Dogs given dry food will drink more water than those fed high-moisture diets, such as canned or frozen foods. Regardless of what type of food he eats, your Australian Shepherd should always have free access to fresh, clean water except within the hour after each meal, when drinking too much could cause serious digestive troubles, such as bloat or gastric torsion/volvulus.

JOIN OUR ONLINE
Club Aussie™

Feeding your Australian Shepherd is part of your daily routine. Have some fun online playing "Feed the Aussie," an exclusive game found only on **DogChannel.com/Club-Aussie**—just click on "Games."

PREVENTING BLOAT

Digestive issues that result in excessive bloating of the stomach can lead to gastric torsion or gastric volvulus, conditions in which the stomach twists, trapping gas and cutting off the blood supply. There has long been a suspected link between a dog's eating a fairly large quantity of kibble, drinking water, and exercising within a short time of each other, but dogs who have done none of these things also bloat, putting this theory up for debate. Nevertheless, most veterinarians recommend not allowing your Aussie to drink large quantities of water, exercise, or be exposed to stressful situations within an hour of meals.

Other ways thought to reduce the risk of bloat include feeding two smaller meals rather than one large meal per day, introducing diet changes slowly to avoid stomach upset, adding digestive enzymes to your dog's food, and avoiding foods containing soybeans, as they usually cause

gas. Should your Aussie seem "burpy" or prone to other digestive issues, the veterinarian may suggest a safe gas-reducing product for him.

The medium-sized Australian Shepherd bloats less often than do larger breeds, such as the Great Dane and German Shepherd Dog, but Aussie owners should be aware of the signs just in case. A dog that acts unusually restless and paces back and forth may be giving early indications of the discomfort associated with bloat, while a dog who repeatedly gags in unsuccessful attempts to vomit and shows swelling in the stomach area is in serious trouble, warranting an immediate trip to the veterinarian or emergency clinic. If not treated immediately, usually with surgery, torsion and volvulus cause death quickly.

LABELS AND LIFE STAGES

The Association of American Feed Control Officials (AAFCO) has set nutritional standards that dog foods must meet before meriting the designation of "complete and balanced." Most commercial foods meet these standards, but that doesn't make all foods equal. Reading labels will help you differentiate between diets that simply meet basic needs and those formulated to keep your Aussie in optimal health. While cost doesn't signify quality, the cheapest diets available simply cannot contain the highest quality ingredients.

Look on the label for the food's ingredients, which are listed in descending order by weight. Quality diets usually list a specific meat source first, sometimes followed by another meat source, and then the remaining ingredients. The first few ingredients comprise a good deal of the total content of the food. Most dry foods contain grain, with sources such as wheat, barley,

Dog foods list recommended feeding portions, with premium-quality diets suggesting smaller amounts due to the greater concentration of nutrients. To determine how much to feed your Aussie, start with the suggested portion for your dog's size and activity level and make adjustments as needed to maintain your dog's ideal weight.

Dogs enjoy the goodness of healthy homemade treats as much as we do. Try these two recipes for extra-special training treats. Refrigerate both when cooled.

Liver "Brownies"

1 pound beef or chicken liver
1 cup cornmeal
1 cup flour (white or whole wheat)
½ cup water
1½ cups wheat germ

Preheat oven to 325 degrees. Puree liver in a food processor. Combine dry ingredients, stir in water, and then add pureed liver and stir until well blended. Pour into nonstick or greased 9- by 9-inch pan. Bake for 22 minutes. Cut into small squares when cool.

Chicken Biscotti

3 cups spelt flour
2½ cups quick oatmeal
1 cup cornmeal
1 cup wheat germ
4 eggs
3 chicken breast halves
1½ cups milk
½ cup chopped parsley

Preheat oven to 350 degrees. Combine dry ingredients and set aside. Grind chicken breasts in a food processor, add the eggs and milk, and run the processor again until mixed. Blend well with dry ingredients and form into an approximately 8- by 14-inch loaf. Place onto a nonstick cookie sheet and bake for 20 minutes, then remove from oven and carefully cut into ¾-inch slices. Turn slices on their sides and bake for an additional 10 minutes.

A quality food for your Aussie's life stage will keep him feeling and looking good.

corn, and others commonly used. For dogs who have difficulty digesting grains or who have grain allergies, grain-free dry foods are becoming increasingly popular.

Protein-to-fat ratios and ingredient

percentages vary depending on the life stage—puppy, adult, or senior—for which the food is formulated. Dry-food ratios differ from wet-food ratios due to the latter's high moisture content, but the ratios prove comparable when analyzed without factoring in the moisture. An average adult dry food's protein-to-fat ratio can be around 22 to 12, with variations depending on the brand and particular diet. A very active herding dog usually needs a diet higher in protein and fat, whereas the reasonably active pet may do better with a more moderate ratio to avoid weight gain.

Puppy diets formulated to support the growth and energy needs of the young dog generally have around a 26 to 16 protein-to-fat ratio on a dry-matter basis (moisture removed), with some higher or lower deviations. Puppy diets also supply

People need to be in charge of their own health, asking questions and finding answers, and we should also do this for our pets. It's time that we take control of what we feed our pets and become educated about their diets.

—Shelley Fritzke, trainer and herding judge from British Columbia, Canada

other nutrients in amounts appropriate for growing youngsters; the aim is to support slow, steady growth to avoid possible skeletal problems caused by rapid growth. Most veterinarians recommend a quality puppy diet for your Aussie until he reaches six months to a year of age.

A senior formula made for a less active older dog may have a protein-to-fat ratio of 16 to 8 or lower to reduce caloric intake and help prevent obesity. These formulas are also said to reduce strain on the older dog's digestive system and other organs that don't function as efficiently as they once did. Because Aussies tend to remain active and energetic longer than many other breeds do, your veterinarian may recommend keeping your dog on a regular adult diet in his senior years.

Whatever your Aussie's age, discuss diet options with your dog's breeder, your veterinarian, your training instructor, and other Aussie owners. In the end, how your dog looks and acts on the chosen food will speak volumes. Healthy skin, a shiny coat, a twinkle in his eyes, and a spring in his step are what we all want for our beloved Australian Shepherds.

Diet Dos and Don'ts

Healthy treats formulated specifically for dogs can be found at every pet-supply shop and make great training aids or occasional "I love you" tokens. Given occasionally so that your Aussie stays trim, treats make us and our dogs feel good. Some human foods also make healthy treats that most dogs love. For example:

- bits of low-fat cheese
- slices of hot dogs
- cooked or raw carrots and asparagus
- plain yogurt (for dogs that can tolerate milk products)
- non-microwave unsalted popped popcorn

Some "people foods" can unfortunately cause your dog serious problems and should be avoided.
- Chocolate contains theobromine and methylxanthines, compounds that may cause vomiting, diarrhea, seizures, and heart arrythmia. The darker the chocolate, the stronger the toxins.
- Fruit seeds and pits from apples,

apricots, cherries, and other fruits can produce cyanide poisoning and can be choking hazards.
- Grapes or raisins can cause kidney failure when eaten in excess. Because the minimum toxic dose for dogs is unknown, it's best to avoid both entirely.
- Just a few macadamia nuts can cause hindquarter weakness or paralysis, muscle tremors, and rapid heartbeat.
- Onions can cause hemolytic anemia in sufficient amounts and are best avoided.

BEAUTY

Good nutrition gives your Australian Shepherd the internal health that really shines through when accompanied by regular grooming. Keeping him glowing with outer and inner beauty isn't difficult, but it does require brushing, nail clipping, ear cleaning, dental care, and other grooming basics. Once your Aussie learns to relax during his grooming sessions and you establish a consistent routine, these quiet times will become shared moments that you'll both enjoy.

"MUST-HAVE" ITEMS

Different brushes serve different purposes. The slicker brush, which has many fine metal pins, catches loose fur and pulls it from the coat; this is a particularly useful tool during the spring and fall shedding seasons, when the Aussie's undercoat "blows out" in handfuls. Many show groomers prefer pin brushes over slickers because the latter can slightly damage the coat; pin brushes usually have rounded

Did You Know?

Having your Aussie's coat shaved off during the summer removes his protection from the sun, leaving his skin susceptible to painful sunburns that can potentially lead to skin cancer. It also makes it easier for flies, mosquitoes, and other biting bugs to make your dog miserable when outdoors.

Gentle brushing is good for your puppy's coat and for building your bond with him.

side through the fur to gently smooth out tiny kinks before using the finer side for finishing. A comb works especially well on the soft fur behind the ears. Combing also helps keep the long fur on the front legs and below the rump—called feathering or furnishings—free of tangles and the debris that can sometimes get caught up in these areas. A flea comb, with very tightly spaced teeth, works fine for catching fleas but not for normal combing.

A quality ear-cleaning solution should be used once a month to remove dirt and wax buildup from your Aussie's ear canals to prevent odor and infection. Because water can remain in your dog's ears and cause trouble, an Aussie that swims frequently may need his ears attended to more often. To aid in keeping your Aussie's mouth healthy, brush his teeth at least every other day with doggy toothpaste. This slows down tartar buildup, massages the gums, and freshens your dog's breath.

Purchasing nail clippers is a must unless you plan to take your dog to the veterinarian or a groomer to have his nails cut or filed down every two weeks. Guillotine-type clippers surround the nail, which fits into an opening above the blade. As you press the handles together, the blade moves and cuts the nail. You can use scissor-type clippers, but if the dog moves unexpectedly during his pedicure, the scissors can cut the dog more easily than the guillotine-type clippers can, as the latter

tips to their bristles. Shedding blades are effective for removing dead coat but must be used carefully to prevent hurting the tender skin underneath. For pet grooming, a slicker for removing loose coat and a pin brush for smoothing out the topcoat usually suffice.

A metal comb with closely spaced teeth on one side and wider spaced teeth on the other allows you to work the wider

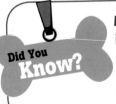

Did You Know?

Many dogs love to roll in things that we consider foul smelling, such as deer droppings, long-dead animal carcasses, and odd-looking piles well beyond recognition. If your Aussie's a "roller," teach a good *leave it* command, watch him closely, and keep some pleasant-smelling shampoo and clean towels at hand.

has a protected blade. Some owners prefer using a small nail grinder that sands the nail quickly and smoothly.

Scissors designed specifically for dog grooming or cutting human hair are better for trimming excess fur around the paw pads than regular all-purpose scissors are. Blunt-ended scissors prove safer for a novice groomer, who may accidentally nick the dog or his or her own hand if the dog moves unexpectedly.

Other necessary grooming supplies include large cotton balls for cleaning ears, shampoo made for dogs, towels for drying off after baths, and, if your Aussie sometimes has runny eyes, tear-stain remover to keep the facial area clean. A blow dryer made specifically for dogs is an optional piece of equipment that dries the coat quickly and blows out loosened fur. You may also want a shower head or spray attachment on a 5- to 6-foot-long hose that you can attach to the bathtub faucet. Many Aussie owners like to use a conditioning spray to make brushing out the coat easier and to add more shine to the coat. Dry shampoos and coat sprays can help clean and freshen the coat in between baths.

GETTING STARTED
Light grooming should start within a few days of bringing your Aussie home, no matter the dog's age. Training a fully coated Australian Shepherd to enjoy grooming can take more time than when starting with a puppy whose fluff doesn't mat or tangle. Unless you adopted a neglected Aussie who needs to be shaved down by a professional to remove severe matting or were lucky enough to adopt an Aussie who already accepts grooming, you should keep initial sessions to no more than five minutes long.

Always make sure that your grooming time is pleasant and positive. Hurried or haphazard introductions to grooming tasks will result in a dog who tries to hide when he sees you pick up a brush or nail trimmer and fusses throughout the entire process. On the other hand, a slow, thoughtful approach produces a dog who happily jumps onto his grooming table in anticipation of some time with and attention from his owner.

Choose a grooming area that's easy to clean, well ventilated, and cool. A grooming table provides a nice height for working on your Aussie, but any stable, sturdy table with a nonslip surface will do. Begin training by getting your dog used to being lifted on and off the table. When he accepts that calmly, briefly hold him on the table and give him a few treats to emphasize that standing there is a good thing. Repeat this several times a day for two or three days.

As your Aussie becomes more at ease on the table, gently brush him and lift each foot as if you were going to cut his nails or trim the excess fur from his footpads. Dogs do not like having their feet handled and will typically balk when you touch them, making this part of the training all the more important to prevent battles later when you want to cut your Aussie's nails dur-

it's a Fact

Mats in your Aussie's coat can trap dirt and moisture against the skin, creating "hot spots" that your dog may bite and chew at, worsening the problem and requiring veterinary attention.

NOTABLE & QUOTABLE

The most important thing about bathing the dog is completely rinsing any product—shampoo or conditioner—out of the coat. Residue left in will not only attract dirt faster, it will also cause the coat to mat at a faster rate.

—Carol Harvey, owner of Lorac's Mobile Pet Spa and
Lorac Australian Shepherds in Aubrey, Texas

ing his routine grooming. However, for the Australian Shepherd not yet accustomed to nail clipping, perfect your technique off the table so that nothing unpleasant happens when he's up there.

Gradually extend the amount of time that your puppy or dog spends on the table while you brush him, handle his feet, look into his ears, inspect his mouth, and do an overall check for any little scrapes or bumps. Give him praise and treats for cooperating. For the restless Aussie, brushing, nail cutting, and other grooming tasks should initially be done in separate table sessions to prevent overwhelming him. As he becomes more comfortable, gradually incorporate most or all of the tasks into one grooming session.

BRUSHING AND TRIMMING THE COAT

Often, an owner will faithfully brush his or her Aussie twice a week but eventually realize that the dog's undercoat is matted down to the skin. This happens when the owner brushes only the surface coat and neglects to move the topcoat aside so that the brush can reach the fur near the skin.

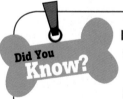

Did You Know? Neglecting to trim the fur between your Aussie's footpads gives your Aussie **less traction on slippery surfaces,** allows him to track more mud and gravel into your house, and enables snow and ice to cling to the feet and cause pain during snowy weather. It also makes the feet much more difficult to clean!

When you brush, start at the neck and gently brush and comb the fine fur behind the ears. From there, work on the main body fur in sections. Place the brush near the skin and stroke outward with the lie of the coat, moving down the sides, back, and rump. Finish by brushing and combing the leg furnishings.

During shedding seasons, your Aussie needs daily brushing with a slicker to remove the loose fur before it becomes tangled up into unsightly and uncomfortable mats that can cause underlying itchy skin infections called *hot spots*. A dog will chew at hot spots and the surrounding areas until they become furless, oozing messes that require medical attention. Once the undercoat sheds out, a thorough brushing once or twice a week should distribute the coat oils evenly, keep the fur mat-free, and allow the skin to breathe so that all stays healthy.

Coated dogs, such as the Australian Shepherd, grow hair that extends below the footpads enough to affect the dog's traction on slippery surfaces and to collect dirt and other debris. This hair should be trimmed flush with the pads once or twice a month, depending on how rapidly it grows. Groomers also trim the fur evenly around the toes and on the back of the pasterns to give the feet and legs a neater appearance, which is something to consider for those who like to keep their Aussies looking sharp.

CLEANING THE EARS

To cleanse your Aussie's ears with an ear-cleaning solution, saturate a large cotton ball with the cleaner and gently rub the inside of the ear, using upward strokes. Don't push the cotton down into the ear; rather, thoroughly clean what you can see.

In hot weather, your Aussie may enjoy an outdoor bath as long as you keep him from rolling in the nearest dirt pile afterward!

Blow drying the Aussie's coat dry after bathing removes loose undercoat, and a small amount of trimming keeps long hairs on the ears and feet neat and mat free. The owner can have this done by a professional groomer, bathe the dog at a groom-them-yourself shop where they have blow dryers, or purchase a dryer and groom the dog at home.

—Kirsten Cole-MacMurray, owner of Toprock Australian Shepherds in Acton, California

Bathing actually "sets" mats into the coat, making them far more difficult to brush out than they would have been prior to wetting your dog.

To prevent a tiny mat from becoming a big problem, thoroughly brush your dog before every bath and gently work any small mats out with a comb and brush or your fingers. Use a detangling spray if necessary.

Naturally, some of the cleaning solution will trickle down the ear canal, loosening dirt and wax that you can't reach, and your dog will expel this as he shakes his head. With regular treatment, only a small amount of dirt should show up on the cotton ball. If the cotton balls come out grimy, and you need to use several to get the ear clean, your dog may have an ear infection or mites and require prescription medication from your veterinarian.

EYE CARE

Though more common in dogs, such as Bulldogs or Pugs, with exaggerated facial structures, Australian Shepherds can experience runny eyes that stain the facial fur an ugly reddish or brownish tone. A fairly heavy eye discharge may relate to diet, allergies, infected tear ducts, or other problems and should be checked out by your veterinarian. In some cases, however, this presents a chronic problem that requires diligent cleaning to prevent a buildup of discharge and to keep the fur looking neat. Ask your veterinarian to recommend an effective product for cleaning around your Aussie's eyes.

HEALTHY TEETH

Flavored doggy toothpastes that appeal to your Aussie's palate can make dental care your dog's favorite part of grooming. Because dogs can't spit out toothpaste like humans do, these toothpastes are made to be safe for your dog to ingest. Toothbrushes designed for dogs have soft, angled bristles that help prevent plaque buildup without damaging the thin outer enamel of the teeth. Some people prefer using fingertip toothbrushes or dental wipes, although the latter doesn't clean between the teeth as well as a brush does.

Before you begin a tooth-brushing routine, train your Aussie to accept having his mouth handled and his teeth inspected. When you feel he's ready, allow your dog to lick a little toothpaste from the brush and then lightly run the brush across his front teeth. Gradually work up to brushing all of the teeth, making sure to include both the outer and inner sides. Brush your Aussie's teeth at least every other day. Understand that even with regular brushing, your dog's teeth may accumulate tartar that requires professional removal, but he will be better off if you stick to a regular home dental-care routine.

DOGGY PEDICURES

Nail clipping can be the most difficult part of grooming. As animals that once depended on healthy feet to live in the wild, dogs are very sensitive about having their feet handled. Before trimming your Aussie's nails on your own, ask your veterinarian to show you how to hold the dog's feet to expose each nail, where to position the nail clippers, and where to cut. Each nail contains a blood vessel, called the *quick*, that stops just short of where you must clip. Cutting into the quick hurts and causes considerable bleeding.

Keep your Aussie still and secure when trimming his nails.

When working with a puppy or dog who is not accustomed to having his nails clipped, work on only one foot in an individual session and gradually build up to doing all four feet at one time. Clip nails only when your Aussie is tired from a good run or vigorous playtime. Initially, try to have someone else hold your Aussie and distract him with treats and petting. Do your best to avoid cutting into the quick, as it will cause your dog to again be hesitant about having his feet touched. If you do hit the quick, use styptic powder to stop the bleeding, wait until your dog calms down, and clip a little off of another few nails so that you end on a happier note.

An alternative that many dogs accept more readily than clippers when introduced to it carefully is the doggy nail grinder. The grinder smooths the nails down to an acceptable length with a small rotary sander. Accustom your dog to the noise of the grinder's motor before use by turning on the grinder and holding it nearby while you feed him treats. Then, with the grinder off, touch the sander to each nail. Once the dog ignores the motor and seems comfortable with the grinder touching his nails, start sanding the nails in very short sessions.

it's a
Fact

The Aussie was selectively bred for an easy-care coat that would be as impervious to weather as possible and could help him withstand both the extreme heat and cold found in the far western regions of the United States, where the breed developed.

Nail clipping is a very important part of regular grooming that's too often neglected. Rescue workers and veterinarians bear witness to stories of untrimmed nails becoming so long that they curve around and grow into the skin. Letting the nails grow just a little too long increases the chance of one catching on something and being ripped off or broken into the quick. Simply taking the tip off of each nail weekly usually keeps them short enough to be comfortable and safe for your dog.

BATHING

The canine's typical dislike for baths is legendary! Many a movie and TV show have humorously depicted the soapy dog squirming his way out of the tub and scrambling through the house, leaving a wet, foamy trail. Though most dogs never really enjoy baths, a proper introduction to the process will make it a more pleasant experience for your Aussie and help prevent a similar scenario from happening in your home.

An owner often waits until his or her dog rolls in something nasty smelling and then plops the poor thing into an unfamiliar slippery basin full of water. To add insult to injury, the dog then must deal with having frothy stuff put all over his body and then having water sprayed or dumped all over him, while through it all his owner tells him to hold still. A proper introduction to bathing takes time, along with generous rewards for cooperation, just as it did when you gradually accustomed your dog to the other necessary grooming tasks.

Your puppy or dog's first time in the tub should be when he's tired. Place a nonslip mat in the tub (if your tub doesn't already have a nonslip surface) and put your Aussie in without running the water. Feed him a few treats to show him that all is well, then

Despite its natural beauty and abundance, the Aussie's coat is relatively easy to keep clean and care for.

lift him out or let him jump out if he is big enough. Repeat this several times over the next few days. Alternate this training with letting him hear and see the water running as he sits outside the tub, earning praise and treats for staying calm. If you plan to use a shower head for rinsing, rest it on the tub floor so the dog can see the water squirting out. Dogs often react worse to spraying water than to flowing water.

When your dog acts comfortable in all of these situations, put him in the tub and turn the water on briefly. Gently hold him in the tub. Give praise and treats when he relaxes, then end the session. Do this a few times until he accepts the running water without much reaction. At that point, lightly spray his side with warm—not hot or cold—water to dampen the coat. Reward for good behavior and then stop. The next time, wet more of his coat, lather up a small area, and rinse well. After this, your dog should be ready for a full bath.

How often you bathe your Aussie depends on your personal preference. With ample brushing, your Aussie's healthy coat and skin should give off little odor, but he won't have that "just-bathed" smell, either. Many quality dog shampoos these days are formulated to gently clean without stripping essential oils from the coat, allowing owners to bathe their dogs more frequently. Of course, a dog that rolls in something foul will need an immediate bath.

To prevent water from getting inside your dog's ears, place a large cotton ball in each ear before the bath. Also be careful not to get shampoo into your dog's eyes. Always rinse the dog thoroughly to avoid leaving any residue behind, which can cause skin irritation. When you are finished rinsing, keep your Aussie in the tub and cover him with a towel to dry him off a bit before he shakes out his coat and drenches you. After he shakes, dry him a little more before you let him out of the tub. You can then finish by blow-drying his coat or putting him in his crate in a draft-free area with several layers of towels.

SKUNKED!

Skunks populate most areas of the United States, which makes a chance meeting between your dog and one of these critters a fair likelihood. Always keep your Aussie current on his rabies shot, as skunks have been known to carry the disease. The most common consequence is that the skunk will spray the dog with an incredibly pungent odor emitted from its rear scent glands.

You will know immediately if your dog has been "skunked," as the odor is very strong. Your Aussie will probably whine and roll on the ground in a pointless attempt to remove the offensive odor. As soon as possible, put on some latex gloves and check your dog to make sure that he wasn't bitten or scratched and thus warrants a trip to the vet. If the odor is the only problem, immediately try to neutralize it with a special shampoo made for this purpose or try a homemade concoction. Your veterinarian or groomer can suggest effective home remedies, or you can try one of these:

- Liberally apply tomato juice to your dog's coat. Let it sit on the coat for a least five minutes, then wash the dog with regular dog shampoo. Repeat several times if needed.
- Mix 1 quart of hydrogen peroxide, ¼-cup baking soda, and 1 teaspoon of liquid soap in a large container. When combined, these ingredients will create a fizzy mixture. Soak your dog, massaging the mixture into his fur. Rinse thoroughly.

Despite your best efforts, it takes weeks for skunk odor to completely dissipate, and the smell becomes most noticeable when your dog gets wet. Some dogs learn to avoid skunks after they've learned their lesson the hard way, but you never know when an unintentional meeting will occur. Keep deskunking shampoo or the ingredients for a homemade remedy on hand, as the sooner you work to neutralize the odor, the better the success rate.

Ask the Groomer

Carol Harvey owns and operates Lorac's Mobile Pet Spa in Aubrey, Texas. Based on her experience as a professional groomer, an Australian Shepherd breeder, and a conformation exhibitor, she answers some questions about correctly grooming an Aussie.

Q. What do you consider the most basic requirements for keeping an Australian Shepherd well groomed?

A. Brushing the Aussie to remove the dead undercoat is the most basic and important part of grooming. Not only does it improve the dog's appearance but it also allows the coat to function properly in protecting the skin from damage and in helping with the cooling/insulating process.

Q. Will bathing a dog with a high-quality dog shampoo rather than a cheaper product or human baby shampoo make a difference?

A. Yes. As with most things, you get what you pay for. For my grooming business, I use only the best I can find, and I usually pay between 40 and 60 dollars a gallon for shampoo. Quality shampoos contain better ingredients and fewer fillers that can irritate the skin. They also tend to thoroughly rinse out easier and clean the dog without completely stripping the skin of needed moisture.

Q. What nail-trimming tips can you give owners?

A. Regular nail trimmers pinch the nail before cutting it, causing mild to severe discomfort, depending upon how close you cut to the quick. I prefer using a [small cordless grinder] with a sanding drum. Even high speed is low enough not to burn, and it allows you to get the nails shorter without damaging the quick.

Q. How do you know when to stop sanding before hitting the quick?

A. There is a dark gel cap around the nerve that can be seen as a darker spot in the center of the toenail as you get close to the quick, and that dark spot lets you know to stop. Work for a second or two on the nail, check the end, and try again if needed. This way, the nails are never painfully injured, and the dog will eventually realize that nail trimming doesn't hurt anymore.

To become a welcome member of society, your Australian Shepherd must receive basic training. An out-of-control dog simply cannot be tolerated in public areas such as walking trails, dog parks, veterinary offices, or anywhere else that people like or need to bring their dogs. A trained dog also makes a better companion in that he doesn't drag you on walks, he comes when called, he sits nicely before greeting people, and he makes you a proud owner overall because you're able to enjoy his company almost anywhere.

Through the years, numerous training methods have been popular. What trainers refer to as the "pop and jerk" method was prevalent for a long time despite the questionable results it produced. In this type of training, the dog was punished for undesired behaviors through repeated collar tugs, but it didn't relay very well to the dog what he was supposed to do, and it often caused more confusion than anything else. Thus trainers started looking for better methods, and reward-based techniques entered the dog-training scene.

Did You Know?

An underexercised Australian Shepherd can build up so much pent-up energy that it affects his ability to learn, much as it would with a child. Ample exercise, both physical and mental, allows your dog to relax and think about what you want him to do.

Trying to teach your young Aussie a new lesson in the middle of a crowded park can be compared to trying to teach a child math on a playground. To teach something new, always start in a quiet, distraction-free area that allows your Aussie to concentrate on the task at hand, then slowly introduce distractions as he progresses.

Reward-based training focuses on what a dog does right rather than on what he does wrong. Using a combination of praise, treats, toys, games, and other things that dogs enjoy, trainers began "marking" desired behaviors by using a device called a *clicker* or by giving a specific verbal cue. Dogs responded remarkably well, and instead of the defeat often produced by punishment methods, they performed commands happily and confidently. Best of all, positive training is easier to administer than punishment-based training, and any owner can learn how to do it.

Many new owners start out training their dogs because they know that they have to, but they end up training their dogs because they enjoy it. Countless competitors in agility, obedience, and other disciplines started out just wanting better-behaved companions. Maybe you'll join them in discovering how much you and your Aussie can accomplish together.

SOCIALIZATION

Though you may not necessarily think of socializing as an aspect of your puppy's training, taking a young Aussie out to meet the world builds the confidence that allows him to retain what he's learned and behave properly when away from his own yard or home. Socialization also strengthens the bond between you and your puppy as he learns to look to you as his leader, as someone to have fun exploring with, and as the person who keeps him safe in all situations.

If you bought your puppy from a responsible breeder, your Aussie has already been introduced to and handled by various people; has had some exposure to household sights, sounds, and smells; and has had the feel of assorted surfaces under his feet. An older puppy or a dog from less fortunate beginnings might require a slower approach to socialization, needing more time to become comfortable around people, other dogs, and life in general than the well-raised puppy, but the overall process works the same with any dog.

Owners were once advised to keep puppies safely at home until around sixteen weeks of age, when the course of vaccinations against serious diseases was complete, but we now know that waiting until a puppy is nearly four months old to begin socializing him bypasses a critical window of time during which it's important to imprint pleasant experiences on him. In other words, what the puppy experiences in the weeks leading up to the four-month mark largely affects how he'll view the world.

An older dog who has not been adequately socialized may bark or growl at what to us seems normal, such as women wearing hats, bearded men, people walking with canes, and so on. Likewise, a puppy who never meets others of his own species won't fully develop the ability to understand canine body language, which is a dog's main method of communication. An unsocialized dog can end up reactive,

The best way to get your Aussie well socialized is to introduce him to different kinds of people and situations. Have him meet a man with a beard, take him to a dog-friendly restaurant, take him for a ride in the car. Go online to download a socialization checklist at **DogChannel.com/Club-Aussie.**

aggressive, or fearful upon meeting other dogs. To become a well-rounded adult, your young Aussie must safely meet different types of people, other puppies, and adult dogs, as well as be exposed to different environments and situations.

To reduce the risk that your puppy will contract a virus before he is fully vaccinated, avoid areas frequented by adult dogs, such as dog parks and pet-supply stores. Instead, bring your puppy along through the fast-food drive-up window, to a friend's house, or even just to a local shopping center to sit outside and watch many different types of people pass by—and probably even say hello. Encourage brief interactions with one or two people at a time, but don't allow a crowd to surround your puppy and overwhelm him. Always keep treats in your pocket and reward your Aussie for nice behavior.

Puppy kindergarten can provide a wonderful means of socializing your pup with other puppies while training him at the same time. As your Aussie learns valuable lessons such as *sit*, *down*, and how to greet

people politely, he will also meet other young dogs and their owners. A qualified instructor will oversee all puppy interactions, allowing them to play together in a group but watching out for bullying or fearfulness. Watch a class in progress before signing up to make sure that you like the instructor and his or her methods. You are looking for someone who gives clear directions with a positive attitude and comes across as a person you can look to for guidance as your puppy grows.

Introducing your puppy to adult dogs can prove more difficult. Dogs adhere to strict greeting rituals that puppies have yet to learn, so most adult dogs cut puppies some slack when they have poor manners. Some, however, do not, and it takes only one bad experience with an intolerant adult for your puppy to get scared or hurt. This makes it vital for your puppy to meet only dogs who you know to be puppy-friendly. A tolerant adult may growl to get a puppy to back off from a toy or bone, but this is a valuable lesson in respect, and no actual harm will befall the puppy.

Always take the lead in ensuring that your Australian Shepherd has pleasant encounters with the world around him. Most puppies go through what trainers refer to as *fear periods* at different developmental stages when they exhibit exaggerated reactions to new or familiar things. In such instances, your puppy will largely draw from your reactions, making it imperative that you remain calm to set a good example for your Aussie around everything you encounter. Be careful that you do not inadvertently reward a fearful reaction by giving the pup a treat or praise in an attempt to soothe him. Wait until your puppy calms down and reward his calm behavior instead.

it's a Fact

Punishment-based methods once prompted trainers to wait to begin training until a puppy could purportedly "handle corrections" at around six months of age. Today's positive-method trainers start teaching puppies as young as eight weeks of age to sit, lie down, come, and perform other behaviors so that obedience becomes an established habit early on.

GOOD-DOG TIPS

Teaching your Aussie to obey basic commands requires know-how, patience, and consistency, but learning new things comes fairly easily to this intelligent, biddable breed. Working with an experienced trainer who uses positive methods moves your training along at a smoother, faster pace because novice trainers often mistake the dog's confusion for stubbornness or disinterest. Communication between trainer and dog needs to be concise with black-and-white clarity; dogs do not understand gray areas.

Use encouragement and motivation when working on cues with your Aussie.

One way that trainers achieve clear communication is by marking the desired behavior at the exact moment it occurs with a clicker or a specific word, such as a clear "Yes." A clicker is a small, handheld box with a metal tongue inside that makes a "click" sound when a button on top is pressed. The trainer clicks at the precise second when the animal performs the desired action and follows the click immediately with a favorite treat—so the click says "Yes," and the treat rewards. Clicker training gained attention as an aid in training killer whales, dolphins, and other mammals for various purposes, such as for exhibition shows at large marine aquariums.

Besides using sound/reward association to encourage the dog to repeat a desired behavior, marker training allows you to break lessons down into small, easily learned steps. For instance, rather than trying to teach a dog how to retrieve in one session, a trainer may click and treat the dog for each small step of the retrieve—touching the dumbbell, reaching for it, taking it into his mouth, holding it, and so on. Working with an experienced clicker trainer, watching a DVD, or reading one of the many books on marker training will help you hone your skills.

In addition to using a marker to tell your Aussie exactly when he's right, there are other things that you can do to make training go more smoothly whether you're teaching your dog to perform a simple *sit* when greeting people or to carry out a three-minute *down/stay* for obedience competition. Consider these training dos and don'ts:

1. **Do always use the same verbal cue for the same behavior.** While this may seem obvious, many owners inadvertently use the same word for different behaviors. For instance, owners often say "Down" to tell the dog to lie down, get off the couch, stop jumping up, and get his feet off the kitchen counter, when it should mean only one of these things.

2. **Don't issue casual commands.** It's easy to become distracted and, without realizing it, repeatedly tell your dog to sit or perform another command without any intention of making sure that the dog complies. This only trains the dog to ignore your cues.

3. **Do stay consistent.** Don't allow your Aussie to jump up on you when you're wearing dirty clothes and then become angry if he jumps on your best outfit. If you never want your dog to jump on you, always insist that he have "four on the floor" before you pet him. This consistency applies to all behaviors.

4. **Do reward randomly for life.** Once a dog learns basic cues, such as *sit*, *down*, and *come*, his owners often fail to reward these behaviors adequately thereafter. In truth, proper responses to your commands need to be reinforced throughout your dog's life. He sits; you greet him. He comes when called; he gets to go for a ride. He lies down; you give him a biscuit. These gestures of positive reinforcement help keep the training in practice.

5. **Don't fight unnecessary battles.** Rather than battle the food hound that constantly tries to get into the trash, block your Australian Shepherd's access to the garbage can. Managing your household so that overly tempting items stay out of your dog's reach makes life easier for everyone in the home.

6. **Don't blame the dog.** When your dog doesn't perform the way you want him to, the problem more often than not lies in your communication. It could be that your timing slightly misses the mark, that you are expecting too much too soon, or that you're inadvertently doing something that confuses your dog. Step back and consider what the problem might be or ask an experienced trainer to help you.

7. **Do have fun.** Keep lessons short and upbeat so that neither of you gets bored.

PUTTING IT ALL TOGETHER

Now that you understand the basics about communicating with your dog and letting him know when he does what you want him to do, you're ready to teach your Aussie some basic cues. Let's take a look at ways to teach some of the most important lessons using what you've learned with a few tricks thrown in.

it's a Fact

Many of today's trainers learned the finer points of clicker training at "chicken camp," as folks affectionately called it, a several-day-long workshop hosted by clicker gurus Marian and Bob Bailey. The Baileys helped people gain the skill, knowledge, and patience needed for animal training by teaching them to clicker-train chickens to perform various behaviors.

With the proper training, your Australian Shepherd will be as well behaved as he is beautiful. One certification that all dogs should receive is the American Kennel Club's Canine Good Citizen (CGC), which rewards dogs who demonstrate good manners. Go to **DogChannel.com/Club-Aussie** and click on "Downloads" to learn about the ten exercises required for your dog to be a CGC.

JOIN OUR
ONLINE
**Club
Aussie**™

The *Sit* Cue

Sit is the most basic exercise. Some dogs sit naturally as they look up at their food bowls; you can mark the behavior and then reward the dog by putting down his meal. Here is a step-by-step approach:

1. Find a quiet room in which to work.
2. Put a treat in your hand and hold your hand at your Aussie's nose.
3. Let your Aussie see and smell the treat, and then slowly raise the treat just above his nose, moving it backward and over his head.
4. Your dog should follow the treat with his eyes and, as he looks up and back, his back end should hit the ground. The instant he reaches the *sit* position, mark the behavior and give him a treat. Some trainers add the word "Sit" at this time, while others wait to introduce the verbal cue until the dog understands what's expected of him.
5. With each subsequent exercise, gradually raise your hand higher, but make the same sweeping gesture as you move your hand back over his head. Say "Sit" and mark and treat each success.

Did You Know?

Dogs read body language very well. Even if you know not to punish your dog when he comes to you, calling him with a stiffened posture, a scowl, and clenched fists shows him that you're angry. Try to relax your body when you call your dog, reward him for coming, and then take a few minutes to calm down before doing anything else.

6. As your Aussie responds readily to the hand gesture and verbal cue, make your hand motions smaller and smaller so that your dog learns to respond to the verbal cue only.
7. Gradually do away with marking the *sit* but add a release word, such as "Free," to tell your dog when he can get up from the position.

If your dog initially jumps up to get the treat, hold it closer to his nose. If he backs up instead of looking up and sitting as your hand moves backward over his head, move into a corner to limit his backward movement.

The *Down* Cue

There are many ways to teach the *down*, but the following method proves successful with most dogs.

1. Work in a quiet room. Position your dog so that he's standing with his back end close to a wall.
2. Put a treat in your hand and hold it at your Aussie's nose.
3. Move the treat (still at your dog's nose) downward toward the floor and back toward your Aussie's belly so that he folds his body into the *down* position. Mark the behavior and treat as soon as his belly touches the floor. You can either begin using the *down* verbal cue now or wait until the lesson becomes more ingrained.
4. Gradually raise your hand higher but maintain the same down-and-back hand sweep combined with the verbal cue. As your dog becomes proficient, slowly phase out the hand signal so that your Aussie understands to perform the *down* on your verbal cue only.

Most cues can be taught with a combination of verbal cues and hand signals.

Even if you mistakenly click when you don't mean to, the dog still earns a treat; it's essential that you hold up your end of the bargain. As long as you don't repeatedly make the same error, the incorrectly marked behavior will end due to lack of continual reinforcement.

—Tracy Mulrenan, a training instructor and canine-sport competitor from Dracut, Massachusetts

If you use positive training techniques, your Australian Shepherd should be looking up at you, eager to learn, whenever you have something new to teach him.

5. Use your release word to tell the dog that he can get up.

Be patient, as it takes some dogs longer to understand the *down*. Praise any movement that your Aussie makes toward the floor and remember to mark at the moment when his belly touches down. If his rear end remains in the air, first mark his belly touching the floor a few times and then wait to mark until he brings his rear down. Always work against a wall, or your dog will likely just back up as you move the treat toward his belly.

The *Stay* Cue

Different trainers favor different ways to teach *stay*. Your Aussie should already be familiar with your release word, and now, instead of releasing your dog as soon as he assumes the *sit* or *down*, you'll teach him to stay by waiting longer to release him, marking each success along the way.

1. Working in a quiet room, stand in front of your dog and tell him to sit. Once he sits, stay close and wait a few seconds before giving the release word. If he holds the *sit*, mark and treat after the release; if he gets up, try again. Don't ask him to hold the position for too long; reduce the amount of time if needed for success.

2. Very gradually work up to longer *stays* with you next to him, marking and treating each success. A verbal *stay* cue isn't necessary because your training is focusing on teaching the dog not to move until he is released, but you can tell your dog to stay if desired.

3. Once your dog holds the *stay* for thirty seconds to a minute with you close by, move one step away, remain there for a couple of seconds, and then step back close to him. Mark and treat success. Note that most puppies won't be ready for a thirty-second *stay* until they are between six months to a year old.

4. Work up to greater distances, but train for duration and distance separately. That means that when you increase distance, keep the time short, and if you increase the time, work at a closer distance. As your dog becomes good at both, slowly combine the two.

5. Repeat these steps with your dog in a *down* position.

Always remember the importance of the release word and never allow your dog to get up on his own. If you become distracted and can't watch him, release him.

The *Come* Cue

Teaching a solid *come* cue (or *recall*) involves two things: always making it pleasant for your dog to come to you and never letting him form the habit of ignoring your command. Here are some tips:

Puppies are sponges when they are young; anything you teach them before sixteen weeks, they will remember for a lifetime. These are the formative weeks, and I try to safely expose them to everything they will see for a lifetime during those weeks.

—Deborah Abbott, a canine-sports competitor from Lebanon, Indiana

A retractable leash keeps steady tension on the collar and gives the dog more distance as he pulls, thus rewarding two behaviors that you want to avoid during leash training. Do not walk your Aussie on a retractable leash until he behaves perfectly on a regular leash.

- Always reward your dog in some way for coming when called. A treat, a game, an ear scratch, a car ride, or something else that he enjoys should invariably follow a recall. If you must call him to put him in his crate or something similar, reward him first.
- Along those lines, never call your dog for anything he finds unpleasant without first offering a highly valued reward. If your Aussie hates baths and you call him to put him in the tub, give him a treat that he loves but gets only at bath time. Never call your dog to punish him.
- Don't teach your dog that he can ignore a recall by calling him when he's off leash and you know he won't respond. If he turns "deaf," when he sees a squirrel in a tree, don't call him to come until you feel confident that your training overrides squirrel patrol.
- Practice outdoor recalls with your Aussie on a 30-foot line in a safe, open area. Cheerfully call him a few times as he walks around and reward him when he complies. If at any time he ignores your call, give a gentle tug on the line, act excited when he looks in your direction, and encourage him to run in for his reward. Occasionally run in the other direction to make catching up with you a fun game for him.

- Have someone else hold your dog as you run away from him, then turn toward him and excitedly call him to you as your helper drops the leash. Reward your Aussie when he reaches you.

Walking on Leash

Teaching your Aussie to walk nicely on leash doesn't happen in a few controlled lessons; you must train him every time he's on leash. Polite on-leash walking differs from the formal heeling seen in competitive obedience, in which the dog maintains his position at his handler's left knee. Most owners want their dogs to be free to sniff and explore the length of a 6-foot-leash while on walks, but they don't want their dogs dragging them along.

If your Aussie is a puppy, never allow him to pull to get where he wants to go, such as over to a person to say hello or across the lawn to sniff a bush. Instead, stop moving and use treats to entice him to stay near you while you walk together toward whatever interests him, then praise him and allow him to explore. Maintain this reward-based control for everything, and he will learn that to get what he wants, he must do what you want—while earning goodies in the process.

When working with an older puppy or an adult who already pulls, eliminate the conflict by putting him in a no-pull halter as well as his regular collar. Attach a separate leash to each and start walking in a familiar area without too many distractions. Rely on the no-pull halter, letting the leash attached to the collar go slack. Reward your dog with a treat and praise when he doesn't pull. Repeat this many times over the next few weeks in gradually more distracting places, always leaving the collar line slack.

Once your dog walks nicely on the no-pull harness, let that line go slack after a few steps and rely on the leash hooked to the collar. The second that your dog pulls, stop dead in your tracks, say "Ah-ah, easy," and switch back to the halter leash. Stopping your forward motion along with switching leashes tells your Aussie that he must not pull no matter where his leash attaches. If he doesn't pull, he earns treats and praise, but if he pulls, he'll be thwarted by the harness. In time, he should learn to walk nicely on a leash and regular collar—but it may take months before this happens.

The *Leave It* Cue

Teaching your dog a *leave it* command prevents from him picking up potentially dangerous items or items that you simply do not want him to put in his mouth. Most dogs learn *leave it* pretty quickly, but it requires constant reinforcement to convince your dog to consistently ignore temptation. Stick some particularly yummy treats and some not-so-yummy ones in your pocket and do the following:

1. Put your dog on leash and place the less-tasty treat on the floor where he can see it but not reach it.
2. As he looks at the treat, say "Leave it" and show him the better treat. When he turns away from the treat on the floor, tell him "Good leave it" and feed him the better treat. Do not let him get the treat that you put on the floor.
3. Repeat this many times in different locations. On walks, keep some of the good treats in your pocket; if your Aussie starts to pick up something questionable, tell him to leave it and give him the treat for obeying.

COUNTERCONDITIONING

The term *counterconditioning* gets thrown about quite a bit in dog training and can be an effective means to resolving minor to serious behavior issues. Counterconditioning involves teaching your Aussie a behavior that is incompatible with an undesirable behavior. For instance, if your dog lunges at passing bicycles on your walking trail, you would set up a scenario in which a bicycle passes at some distance away. The moment your dog spies the bicycle (but before he reacts to it), tell him to sit and then strongly reinforce that *sit* cue with treat after treat until the bicycle has passed out of sight.

Have the bicycle gradually come closer and closer until it can pass by while your dog maintains that highly reinforced *sit* position. If he sits, he can't lunge and has therefore learned a behavior that "counters" the undesired behavior. More complicated than it sounds, counterconditioning also involves desensitization, proper timing, and an understanding of how to gradually fade reinforcement. It often includes the assistance of a professional trainer to increase your odds of success.

BEHAVIOR

Discipline in dog training doesn't involve punishment; instead, it is a combination of training and management that ultimately teaches your Australian Shepherd the self-control, or self-discipline, to resist chewing up throw pillows, jumping on people, stealing food from the table, and engaging in other behaviors that seem perfectly reasonable and fun to him but that we humans find unacceptable. By establishing rules and consistently enforcing them while we teach our Aussies the behaviors that we find acceptable, peace reigns in the household.

Sadly, many people become so frustrated with their dogs' problem behaviors that they eventually give up and turn their dogs over to rescue groups or shelters. Some behaviors prove easier to resolve than others, but knowledge and determination can enable an owner to overcome almost any problem. Many owners who really want to keep their dogs ultimately enlist the help of professional trainers only to discover how intelligent and willing to please their Aussies really are. A trainer can translate the owner's wants to the dog,

Did You Know?

Dogs do not act out of spite, revenge, or malice; they act on their desires of the moment until they are mature enough to practice the necessary self-control to do what their owners train them to do rather than simply what is fun for them.

You can help your puppy or dog learn self-control by asking for trained obedience behaviors during the excitement of a game. Rather than throw the ball immediately after your Aussie returns it to you, ask for a split-second *sit* and then reward him by starting the game again. Gradually add in other commands as his self-control increases.

while at the same time showing the owner how to communicate in terms that the dog can understand, allowing dog and owner to arrive at an understanding that enriches both of their lives.

CHEWING

Just as we like to touch interesting objects with our hands, puppies use their mouths and noses to explore the world and consequently pick up countless items along the way, many of which you would prefer they leave alone. Puppies also experience pain and discomfort from teething between two and five months of age, which compels them to chew on things to give their sore gums some relief. An underexercised or lonely Aussie may also chew to occupy his mind and alleviate boredom.

With so many reasons to pick up items and chew on them, it becomes obvious why chewing and the destruction that accompanies it rank highly on the list of problems that cause owners to relinquish their dogs. An owner may become upset after mistakenly concluding that his or her Aussie chewed up the Persian rug out of spite, but in reality the puppy simply found something to do while his owner

was gone. Instead of getting angry, the correct reaction is to rethink leaving an unattended puppy loose where he can do damage and to instead safely confine him to a secure area, such as his crate.

Puppy-proofing proves imperative when raising a young Aussie or bringing home a rescue dog who may have issues. Your belongings cannot be chewed to pieces if they are stored safely away and you supply your Aussie with a variety of quality doggy chew toys. Nylon bones are available in an assortment of sizes, flavors, and styles. There are toys that you can fill with treats, such as peanut butter or pieces of kibble, that will keep your Aussie's jaws occupied and entertain him as he works to get at the food inside.

When not crated, your new Aussie needs supervision at all times, as serious damage can happen very quickly. If your dog does manage to sink his teeth into something inappropriate, gently tell him "No" and then playfully but purposefully redirect his attention to a suitable chew toy. This "don't-do-that-do-this-instead" feedback offers the black-and-white clarity that speeds training along.

Trading with your Aussie is very effective in convincing him to give up one item for another once he learns that complying results in a reward. The premise is simple: offer your Aussie something that he values more highly than whatever he has. If he picks up a sock, offer his favorite toy in exchange as you say "Give." When he's playing with that favorite toy, which he may be reluctant to release, offer him a high-value treat in exchange as you tell him "Give." This approach teaches your Aussie to happily give things up so he never feels conflicted when you take things from him. Never wrestle with your

Owners inadvertently encourage nipping by playfully grabbing the puppy's nose, which leads to play biting. Similarly, chasing is encouraged when children teasingly run away from the puppy and laugh as he chases them. Attention-seeking behaviors, like nudging and pawing, are rewarded when you respond by petting or playing with the puppy. You must always consider where a behavior might lead.

—Mary Jo Stabinski-Heckman, owner of Paws 4 Thought in Eagleville, Pennsylvania

dog over an item; he may think that you're playing a fun tug game, or it could create avoidable possessiveness issues.

NIPPING

Nipping is another problem that stems from the canine's desire to mouth things. In an eight-week-old puppy, nipping may seem cute, but jaw strength increases very quickly as your Aussie grows, and soon those sharp puppy teeth hurt like the dickens. If not stopped early on, nipping in an Aussie puppy can progress to herding-type behaviors, such as nipping at people's ankles or bodies to "move them along" as he would do with cattle or sheep. The nips hurt, but they are not aggressive and they don't originate from fear or pack-rank issues. A herding dog's nips nevertheless may leave bruises and can be a real problem around children.

Prevention offers the best solution. When your puppy nips at your skin or hair, give him a firm "No," try to turn his attention toward an acceptable toy, and praise him when he takes the toy. If he persists in nipping, again tell him "No" and stop interacting with him for a couple of minutes. Your puppy will likely respond well when

he makes the connection that nipping and hearing "No" means the end of the game, much as it did when he elicited a yelp from a littermate, and their mom moved in to enforce a brief time out.

If you adopted an older puppy or dog with an established nipping problem related to his herding instinct, a firm "No" along with adequate mental stimulation and ongoing obedience training to establish and maintain control should help your dog adapt to the no-nipping rule. As always, ample physical exercise takes some of the edge off with this energetic breed. For a persistent nipping problem, you may need assistance from an experienced trainer.

WHINING

Puppies or adult dogs sometimes whine when they don't feel well, so constant whining calls for a trip to the veterinarian. Most times, though, whining means that your Aussie feels insecure, lonely, bored, or a combination thereof, and he wants you to make those bad feelings go away. Taking him out of his crate every time he whines, for example, only reinforces his whining, so you must steel yourself once you've ruled out an actual problem.

Be aware of some of the causes of whining, most of which have simple fixes. If your Aussie feels isolated, place his crate in a location where he can see family activities. If his crate is near a heating/cooling vent, he may be too warm or chilly, so check the temperature in your dog's area. Most puppies and dogs like soft bedding that they can curl up on or in, so make sure that your Aussie has adequate bedding. A puppy may whine when he needs to go out to relieve himself; remember, a very young puppy can't hold it for more than an hour or two during active daytime hours.

it's a Fact

Your dog doesn't hang his head and act apologetic when you come home to a destroyed couch because he knows he did something wrong; instead, he is responding to your angry body language and tone of voice and hopes to placate you through submissive behaviors.

An Aussie of any age may whine if he feels that he's not getting enough attention; he needs plenty of exercise and interaction with his family, even if he's just joining everyone on a car ride. Your Aussie may whine out of boredom, and while this can't be completely avoided during crate time, you can help alleviate it by rotating his assortment of safe toys daily.

EXCESSIVE BARKING

Dogs bark for a variety of reasons: to alert the family to intruders, to gain attention, to let everyone know that a squirrel ran up the tree, and more. Most owners appreciate the barking that tells them when someone's approaching the house or when a questionable character keeps hanging around outside, but barking becomes a problem when the dog sounds off about everything that moves or makes noise. Many a friendship between neighbors has been strained when one of them acquires a dog that barks constantly.

Excessive barking usually results from boredom. Dogs enjoy barking—it passes the time, it burns off energy, and it taps into the herding breed's heritage of vocalizing to help move stock. Once again, adequate exercise, mental stimulation through training, and fun times with you decrease the chances that a barking problem will develop. Most dogs bark when they are left alone outside in a kennel or yard, so don't leave your dog unattended outdoors for long periods of time. Utilize landscaping or privacy fencing to block barking triggers, such as the neighbor's squirrel feeder, from your dog's view.

Mixed messages, such as praising your Aussie for barking when a stranger comes to the door but yelling at him when he barks at the mail carrier every day, will only confuse him. To your dog, the mail carrier

Never allow your Aussie to run the fence line, barking at passing motorists, joggers, or bicycles, as once this behavior becomes established, it can be very difficult to stop. As soon as you notice him keying on someone or something, tell him "Leave it" and call him to you for a game or a few treats.

represents the ultimate "intruder" who he bravely "scares away" daily. If you want your dog to alert you to people approaching, you must be consistent and let him alert you no matter who it is. You can, however, teach your dog to quiet down on command once you know all is safe.

Most trainers teach a *speak* command rather than trying to quiet an already keyed-up dog in a barking frenzy. Teaching *speak* and *quiet* cues defines each action to the dog and therefore provides clarity. Teaching a vocal dog to speak usually comes easily—get him a little excited about a toy, say "Good speak" after the first little woof, and then reward him with the toy. It's usually unnecessary to mark this behavior because the dog loves to bark, which makes this training self-rewarding.

After a few repetitions, mark the moment he stops barking (even if his mouth is full of toy), say "Good quiet" to build word association, and reward him with a high-value treat. You need to mark this behavior to strongly reinforce it because your dog will not find quieting down self-rewarding. After many repetitions, tell your dog "Quiet" without giving him the toy, wait until he stops barking, and mark. Gradually require more quiet time before the marker, and eventually phase out the marker altogether.

BEGGING

It happens all the time—a lovely sit, an expectant half-open mouth, a slight twist of the head, and soulful staring eyes; next thing you know, you're sharing your ham sandwich with that masterful beggar, your Aussie. Every time you give in and offer your dog a bite of your food, you reinforce what eventually becomes an annoying, difficult-to-stop habit that was best never started in the first place. As with many problems, if you never encourage begging, your Aussie won't learn that it reaps rewards.

Once you have a beggar on your hands, you have the choice of confining your dog any time you eat or bracing yourself to resist the beggar's tricks and keep your food for yourself. In the latter instance, your dog will no doubt push a bit harder as he becomes frustrated over not getting his perceived share (which, in his eyes, would be all of it), but you must remain strong and ignore his pleading eyes. In time, and it may take months, your dog will figure out that you no longer share your food and that he receives treats in other situations, such as when he's learning new things.

Counter surfing becomes a problem with a dog who can reach food items on the kitchen counter or table and thus finds his efforts rewarded. Prevention means eliminating the reward by keeping food out of your Aussie's reach and always supervising him at times when you need to have food out on the countertops or table. Some trainers recommend using a deterrent—such as a shaker can that will make a startling noise if the dog puts his feet on the counter and knocks into it—in the hope that it will teach the dog the error of his ways, but success with this method varies. Because hot food can

Your Australian Shepherd can be persuasive, but don't let his tricks sway you into giving him food from your plate.

For some dogs, running loose with multiple dogs in a dog-park setting or at a doggy day care can bring forth otherwise unseen aggression, fearfulness, or bullying. If your dog seems to prefer your company to that of other dogs, accept it and work on your disc-catching, agility, or other interactive skills.

injure your dog, and some "people foods" can make your dog sick, prevention offers the safest solution.

JUMPING UP

If you ever watch dogs interact with each other, they engage in a lot of face-to-face greetings that they try to carry over to humans, which explains why your Aussie jumps up on you when saying hello—he wants to get closer to your face. While many owners don't mind this when in their yardwork clothes, most find it less appealing when dressed in business attire for an important meeting. The trouble is, a dog cannot differentiate between frayed jeans and a new Armani suit, so teaching your dog never to jump on you or anyone else is the best bet.

From the day you bring your puppy or dog home, pet him only when he has all four feet on the floor. Trainers usually recommend insisting that a dog sit before being petted, and while this is wise because it gives your dog a specific action to perform, it seems to be a rule that many owners find difficult to follow. As long as you and anyone else greeting your dog maintain absolute consistency, requiring four feet on the ground works just about as well. Keep in mind that any time you or

someone else pets your dog after he jumps up, your dog has been rewarded for this undesirable behavior.

Because the *down* cue tells the dog to lie down, jumping up should be met with an *off* cue followed by your placing the dog's feet back on the ground. Wait a second or two to make sure that he doesn't jump up again, and then quietly tell him what a good dog he is as you pet him.

Avoid using an excited tone of voice when you greet your dog, as that excites him even more and encourages him to release that excitement by jumping up. For the very excitable dog, prepare a treat-stuffed rubber toy in advance to offer him when you get home. This will distract him long enough to calm down, and then you can enjoy a relaxed hello.

DIGGING

Watching a dog gleefully dig after a mole or some other critter drives home how much the canine species enjoys digging. Digging not only gives your Aussie something fun to do but it also provides exercise and brings out all of those wonderful earth smells that we mere humans cannot detect. Natural as it may be, digging creates unattractive and unsafe holes throughout the yard, ruining your landscaping and creating hazards. Though Australian Shepherds don't necessarily dig as wholeheartedly as some other breeds, such as terriers, do, they will dig out of boredom or to chase after underground rodents.

Obviously, making sure that your yard is free of burrowing animals is a key factor in preventing digging. Of course, providing ample exercise and attention forestalls the boredom that often results in digging. Supervising your Aussie outdoors also helps you catch your dog as soon as his paws get

NOTABLE & QUOTABLE

Digging is a natural behavior. Dogs dig for grubs under the soil, to expose damp earth to lie on in hot weather, or just because it is fun! We can interrupt digging behavior by calling the dog and giving him something else to do, such as chase a ball, or we could simply designate a yard area as dog digging heaven.

—Maggie Blutreich, charter member of the Association of Pet Dog Trainers and owner of BRAVO! Force Free Training near Charlotte, North Carolina

Consider barricading your flowerbeds to help your Aussie resist the temptation to dig there.

your Aussie to happily dig up. If he starts digging somewhere else in the yard, tell him "No dig" and take him to his digging area. A little fence with a gate around the area can be used to prohibit access during especially muddy times or when you want your Aussie to stay clean.

COPROPHAGIA

Most commonly found in puppies six months to a year of age, coprophagia (the act of eating stool) understandably disgusts even the most dedicated dog person. Suggested reasons for the behavior include dietary deficiencies, lack of fiber intake, inadequate enzyme activity, and others, but no definite explanation exists. Feeding your Aussie a high-quality premium diet sometimes helps, as does adding an enzyme supplement to his food, but no particular change in diet is guaranteed to put a stop to this behavior.

Numerous companies offer dog-food additives or products to sprinkle on the feces to make it taste bad, and sometimes these work. Most times, however, the puppy must simply outgrow the habit, and keeping the yard free of waste becomes the only surefire preventive. This means cleaning up immediately after your puppy defecates each and every time, as it's believed that the fewer times this behavior occurs, the less likely it is to become a lifelong habit.

going, allowing you to issue a sharp "No dig!" and diverting his attention toward an acceptable activity. Also try placing some of your dog's waste into a started hole to deter further digging.

For the ardent digger, consider setting aside an obscure area as a digging zone, even lightly burying washable toys for

Did You Know? Responding to food aggression by forcefully taking away your dog's food only substantiates that he needs to worry when you approach his food and, consequently, increases his aggression. Seek professional help from an experienced non-force trainer who can show you how to eliminate your dog's anxiety around food and his aggression.

Punishing a dog for coprophagia has proven ineffective. If anything, your dog will learn to hide from you while he eats poop, but the problem will persist. Should the problem linger as your puppy grows up, or should you adopt an Aussie with an already established habit, talk to your veterinarian for suggestions on how to stop it. In the meantime, train a solid *leave it* command and plan on picking up after your dog as soon as he makes a deposit.

AGGRESSION

Aggression represents the most difficult and dangerous problem seen in our canine companions. A dog's aggressive reaction can result from issues such as poor socialization, resource guarding, frustration, fright, sexual behavior, prey drive, and pack-rank issues, and it can be directed toward you, family members, other people, or other animals. Unacceptable no matter the reason, aggressive behavior can more easily be resolved when a professional trainer intervenes before the behavior escalates.

Aggressive displays take various forms, from a hard stare or quick turn of the head to a snap or eventual bite. Most aggressive behaviors in dogs can be avoided by following basic training advice: establish consistent rules; train with positive methods rather than with punishment, which can evoke aggression; and maintain the position of a strong leader through kindness and control. Avoiding or ignoring aggressive behavior, such as food possessiveness, in hopes that it will go away only intensifies the problem and makes for a slower resolution.

Don't rely on the advice of just anyone to resolve an aggression problem; seek the help of a professional trainer who comes highly recommended for his or her ability to work with aggressive dogs. The average person isn't trained to read canine behavior signs. For instance, many people believe that a wagging tail indicates friendliness, but a moving tail can actually be part of an aggressive stance that says "back off." Reading the dog's body language incorrectly could result in a bite.

Owners sometimes mistake play behaviors for aggression, as many dogs "play growl" when they grab a ball or pull on a tug toy. If you deal with this innocent behavior harshly, you could create aggression where none existed. It's better to have a trainer observe your Aussie and tell you that your dog's just playing rather than to handle his behavior incorrectly and hurt your relationship with your dog. In short, it's best to talk to someone experienced in working with aggression problems.

MOUNTING

Often considered a sexual behavior, a dog's mounting another dog usually occurs as an attempt at control, to get attention, or in response to stress. When dealing with an intact male and a female in season, the behavior does relate to sexual arousal, but the mounting so often seen between male dogs surfaces as a display of dominance or as a reaction to the heightened state of excitement brought about by running and wrestling during play—the dog responds in the way that his body tells him to without really thinking about why. Though normal among dogs, mounting can result in aggression in ill-matched interactions.

When the recipient of this attention is an older, confident male and the offender is a youngster who is learning the finer points of doggy etiquette, the adult may growl to make the young dog back off. The young dog should act appropriately submissive, and the two dogs will either separate or begin playing again. If, however, mounting happens between two adult males and the recipient takes unkindly to the other dog's disrespect, a fight can ensue. Because these competitive issues are largely hormone driven, neutering can help prevent or reduce mounting between dogs.

If you adopt an adult Aussie with an established problem of mounting other dogs, your goal should always be to divert your dog's attention before he mounts and remove him from the situation long enough for him to calm down. If your dog acts aggressively toward you or the other dog as you approach, seek professional help. Also understand that not all dogs play well with others. Sometimes a game of fetch with you presents a safer option for playtime.

Mounting people's legs ranks as one of the most embarrassing canine behaviors for the dog's owner, and one that is extremely unappreciated by guests. Some dogs mount to garner attention, and it certainly works, but other dogs consider it a show of control and can even act aggressively when you or the dog's "target" tries to pull or push him away. If the dog acts aggressively, it means that rank issues exist in your household and that you need professional help to establish a proper relationship with your dog and gain the necessary control to avert aggression.

For the attention-seeking mounter, you can issue a command to counter the mounting behavior; for example, require the dog to sit when greeting people. Or, because mounting usually happens amid the initial excitement of your guests' arrival, give the dog a treat-dispensing ball or other toy to occupy him as guests arrive and allow him to say hello after he calms down. In time, he may forget about mounting people. In extreme cases, a squirt of water from a clean spray bottle may discourage this unwanted attention.

Both intact and altered dogs, males and females alike, will hump pillows or other soft items. As long as this behavior doesn't become obsessive, it's perfectly normal. However, you probably want to teach your Aussie to leave your pillows alone and offer a designated pillow or stuffed toy in a more private location so that your dog doesn't embarrass you, your family, or your guests.

SEPARATION ANXIETY

A dog suffering from separation anxiety basically freaks out when his owner leaves him alone, often causing himself personal injury as well as destroying household items, chewing on the door frames, pawing at the walls, or engaging in other desperate and destructive behaviors. Less experienced trainers or owners often misdiagnose poor training, inadequate exercise, or other related problems as separation anxiety because the dog soils in the house or tears things up when left alone.

An adolescent Aussie left loose in the house when his owners are out may well destroy the couch cushions because he's not mentally ready for that kind of freedom and because it passes the time in an active, fun way. While this behavior is a product of being left alone, it relates more to a lack of supervision and a lack of the self-control that prevents the better-trained and more staid adult from engaging in such activities. In short, this dog was given too much unsupervised freedom too soon.

Serious cases of real separation anxiety, in which the dog is at risk of serious injury and causing severe destruction, should be worked on under the guidance of a professional trainer. Separation anxiety can often be seen in rescue dogs, particularly those who've bounced around between several homes. Such a dog sometimes attaches very strongly to one or two people and needs help to understand that being away from his special people doesn't mean that he isn't safe or that he will once again be deserted.

A milder case of separation anxiety, in which the dog simply whines and perhaps barks for a while after you leave, can sometimes improve when you make your exit a very casual process and distract the dog as it occurs. For instance, if you go to your dog's crate and tell him how sorry you are for leaving before you exit the house every day, he will pick up on your tone of voice and worry as you walk out the door; you are inadvertently encouraging your dog to be anxious. If, on the other hand, you hand him a rubber toy with something delicious hidden inside as you nonchalantly leave, the event becomes a happy one. Coming back home should be approached in a similar low-key manner to again help your dog remain calm and start perceiving your comings and goings as no big deal.

Ideally, this type of training starts in your Aussie's puppyhood. Because he must relieve himself very frequently when young, he adjusts to being left alone in the crate for short periods of time early on, and gradually these periods extend to a few hours at a time. This slow adjustment helps most dogs avoid separation issues, as long as crate time is age appropriate and reasonable. Any dog that spends most of his time in a crate or other confined area will very likely display problem behaviors.

Some dogs respond well to verbal cues as their owners leave—something like "I'll be back." The verbal cue tells them that their people will return and thus offers reassurance. If you do use a verbal cue as you leave, say the words matter-of-factly so as not to cause anxiety. Train your Aussie by initially leaving for short periods of time; for example, to run to the mailbox. Keep your return equally low-key; a simple "I'm home" as you peruse the mail suffices and encourages your dog to stay calm when you enter the house. Be careful to extend your time away gradually so that your dog doesn't become anxious about your arrival.

Your Australian Shepherd hails from hardy working ancestors, making him an energetic dog with an innate need to participate in daily activities. If you could ask your Aussie whether he'd rather join you on the couch to watch television, go for a 5-mile hike, or run an agility course, his answer might be, "Let's go for the hike this morning, run the agility course in the afternoon, and relax on the couch this evening." In short, your Aussie may be perfectly content to spend quiet time together, but he wants to do something active first.

While your dog would love spending all day doing things with you, most Australian Shepherds make do with a couple of good runs in a fenced-in area combined with a rousing game of fetch or Frisbee each day. Throw in some basic obedience—such as insisting on a sit before throwing the ball—to reinforce control during these games, and you've added important mental stimulation. When an owner doesn't provide adequate physical and mental activity, an Aussie can become restless, destructive, noisy, and generally annoying due to boredom and pent-up energy.

Doing things with your Aussie benefits you, too, by keeping you active. Your Aussie will enjoy activities such as disc-catching, flyball, agility, tracking, skijoring, and more, and it will get you moving with your dog. For those interested in less physically demanding activities, taking your Aussie on therapy visits to nursing homes or hospitals can be very satisfying. You are sure to find an activity that suits both you and your dog.

OBEDIENCE

Every dog requires some obedience training to learn the basics needed for a mannerly companion dog. Various organizations, such as the American Kennel Club (AKC), United Kennel Club (UKC), and the Australian Shepherd Club of America (ASCA), expand upon these basic commands in competitive obedience by coordinating specific exercises that handler and dog must perform accurately to earn titles. Building on and progressing beyond the basic commands that most dogs learn, competitive obedience demands quick responses to cues, precision execution, and skillful handling.

In competition, handlers cannot encourage their dogs with gestures or voice cues other than the exact signals or verbal commands allowed in the rules. Each dog starts with a perfect score, and the judge deducts points for faults in the team's performance. While it may sound rather stifling, competitive obedience presents a wonderful training experience for anyone of any age who believes in positive training methods and has an appreciation for working toward a standard of excellence.

Each handler-and-dog team must earn a qualifying score three times at a given level to earn the title offered at that level, and the levels become increasingly difficult as exercises such as retrieving and scentwork enter the scene. Initially, your dog will perform some work on leash, but most competitive obedience exercises are done off leash. Heeling, in which the dog remains in position by the handler's left leg as the pair moves at different speeds in unison, can be incredible to watch when done smoothly and is an important part of each level of competition.

The Aussie's quick mind and desire to work are well suited to competitive obedience, and the breed boasts more than its share of top-level titles. Fun training that imprints obedience exercises can start when your puppy is as young as eight weeks old, but the adult rescue dog is certainly capable of becoming an obedience champion, too. The older Australian Shepherd enjoys learning as much as the youngster does. Local training clubs and private trainers can get you started in competition-style obedience training and guide you through this enjoyable and demanding sport.

RALLY

After becoming an AKC titling sport in 2005, rally is now also hosted by several other organizations and has become tremendously popular, thanks to the sport's more informal approach to obedience. In a rally competition, signs are placed around the course, and each sign specifies an obedience exercise that the handler and dog must perform before moving on to the next sign, or station. Weaving around cones, performing 270-degree turns, and pivoting in place are just a few examples of

The fast pace, quick thinking, and athletic ability required for success in agility are right up the Aussie's alley.

the exercises that can be found on the rally course. The exercises become gradually more difficult as handler-and-dog teams progress through the levels, but rally success is within the reach of novice trainers.

Though teams must perform all of the exercises correctly, part of rally's appeal comes from the fact that you can talk to your dog while competing. Precision takes a back seat to team spirit as judges look for the dogs' enthusiastic responses to their handlers' cues. Smiling faces and wagging tails punctuate most performances because both handlers and dogs enjoy the relaxed interaction in pursuit of titles. Because of the sport's popularity, most obedience clubs and many professional trainers offer rally classes to those who've mastered basic obedience commands.

AGILITY

Agility presents physically and mentally demanding challenges that require your Aussie to be in tip-top shape as he negotiates an obstacle course under your direction within an allotted time period. Obstacles include an A-frame, weave poles, different types of jumps, tunnels, and more that put the Aussie's brainpower and athleticism to work, much to this breed's enjoyment. Numerous owners and their Aussies have earned top-level titles from one of the many organizations that offer agility, including the AKC, the UKC, the United States Dog Agility Association (USDAA), and the North American Dog Agility Council (NADAC).

Experienced trainers begin teaching basic agility behaviors to puppies but do not work on extreme physical activities, such as jumping or climbing full height, until the dogs have finished their growth phase to avoid damaging developing joints or muscles. For those who adopt rescue dogs, many trainers recommend agility to help build the dog/owner bond as well as increase the dogs' confidence. Anyone who has witnessed a dog's obvious delight at conquering an obstacle that he had previously been unsure about understands how agility can impart an "I'm-all-that" attitude to the dog.

In a similar fashion to other canine sports, each dog-and-handler team starts with a perfect score and loses points for performance faults by either the dog or the handler. Each level adds more obstacles in increasingly difficult sequences with fewer faults allowed to earn a qualifying score. With continued training, most teams reach the point at which the dog responds to the slightest movement from the handler, creating an exciting partnership that is breathtaking to watch but can be truly appreciated only when experienced firsthand. Many training centers and private trainers, likely at least one in your area, offer agility lessons.

FLYBALL

Flyball is as good as it gets for an Aussie who's a tennis-ball-retrieving fanatic. This sport is a relay race in which teams of four dogs compete against each other. Each canine team member runs down a lane, clearing four hurdles on the way to a box that ejects a tennis ball via a release pedal. The dog pounces on the release pedal, catches the flying tennis ball, and returns back over the hurdles to his handler at the starting line, at which point the next dog is released. The hurdles are set at a height appropriate for the team's shortest dog. Teams race two at a time, with the team completing all four runs in the fastest time winning that heat.

The Australian Shepherd's speed, agility, and drive have made the breed a longtime favorite in flyball, a fact evidenced by the number of Aussies earning titles according to statistics kept by the sport's governing organization, the North American Flyball Association (NAFA). Though dogs must be trained to stay on course and not to interfere with other dogs, flyball training mainly focuses on speed, teaching the dog to catch the ball, and teaching the dog how to turn at the box without straining his body. Because the handlers stay at the starting line, flyball offers an excellent opportunity for less active owners to compete in an exciting sport.

It's more difficult to find flyball classes than it is to find instruction in agility or obedience, but those involved in flyball say it's worth searching for someone to train with or even buying or building your own box and forming a team. If interested in this dynamic activity, contact NAFA for information on how you and your Aussie can get started.

FREESTYLE

Canine freestyle, or "dancing with your dog," involves a beautiful blending of obedience and dance showcased in choreographed performances by handler-and-dog teams. Performed in a large open ring, freestyle routines can include spins, bows, high fives, leg kicks, and more. These dance moves are executed in harmony with the handler's chosen song, which can come from any genre of music. Handlers often wear costumes, with their dogs wearing matching collars or scarves.

Canine Good Citizen

The AKC Canine Good Citizen, or CGC, test evaluates your Aussie on how he performs ten different exercises to see if he displays a stable temperament, good manners, and basic obedience training. The socialization and training discussed in previous chapters sets your dog up for success, although you may want to enroll in a CGC training class to ensure that your dog behaves politely and seems comfortable with the test's ten steps:

1. **Accepting a friendly stranger.** Your Australian Shepherd must behave politely while you greet an unknown person.
2. **Sitting politely for petting.** Your dog should quietly accept petting from an unknown person.
3. **Appearance and grooming.** The tester will gently check your dog's ears, pick up his feet, and lightly brush him, all of which your dog must accept good-naturedly.
4. **Out for a walk.** Your Aussie must exhibit good leash manners as you walk around.
5. **Walking through a crowd.** You must show that you have control over your leashed dog as you walk past several people; your dog may show interest but should not pull toward or show fear of anyone in the crowd.
6. **Performing *sit* and *down* positions on command and staying in place.** Your Australian Shepherd must perform a *sit*, *down*, and *stay* at the tester's command.
7. **Coming when called.** Your dog must stay as you walk 10 feet away and then come to you when called.
8. **Reaction to another dog.** With your dog on leash, you approach another handler and dog, chat a moment, and move on; your dog should show no more than a casual interest in the other dog.
9. **Reaction to distraction.** The tester will evaluate your dog's reaction to a distraction, such as a sudden loud noise or a jogger; your Aussie can show a slight reaction but should recover quickly.
10. **Supervised separation.** You move out of your dog's sight for three minutes as someone else holds his leash; he should not show more than mild nervousness or worry during this time.

Safely start your puppy's agility training at home using treats to lure him across a 10- to 12-inch-wide board with its ends placed on pieces of two-by-four to mimic the dogwalk. Then put the same board on the ground with a two-by-four under the middle to let your puppy feel movement under his feet similar to what he'll encounter on the teeter.

Freestyle offers a fun alternative to traditional obedience and is especially appealing to those who like to move to music. If you have an interest in dance, you can adapt a routine to suit your particular skills and train your Aussie accordingly. You might find that your dog expresses a quiet opinion about the music, as competitors invariably say that their dogs show more enthusiasm for some tunes than others. So if you like Bach, but your dog's more the Aerosmith type, just go with it.

The World Canine Freestyle Organization and the Canine Freestyle Federation offer competitive titles at levels from beginner to advanced. Those who are unsure about the idea of people dancing with their dogs to music clearly have yet to see the training and teamwork exhibited in canine freestyle. The dog's quick responses to a range of cues, combined with attentive heeling and a happy attitude, should be what every competitive handler works for in his or her performance.

TRACKING

All dogs use their noses to explore the world, and we humans can never imagine how much a dog can glean from sniffing a single bush on a hiking trail. Putting this marvelous sense of smell to work for us through the sport of AKC or ASCA tracking gets owner and dog outdoors, often during the crispness of the morning dew, to take advantage of ideal trailing conditions. Many multisport competitors hail tracking as their favorite, thanks in part to the many quiet times in nature shared between owner and dog during training.

To earn a title, your Aussie follows the tracklayer's scent from start to finish on a track that meets the competition level's requirements for length and difficulty. Articles of a specific material, type, and size are dropped along the trail, and your dog must find these articles and indicate his finds with a consistent behavior, such as lying down or picking the items up. Titling levels increase in difficulty from open fields to heavy cover and to city terrain such as concrete, asphalt, and gravel.

Because tracking focuses on a skill that your Aussie already possesses—scenting—training simply works toward turning that skill to the desired scent. To get started, you might walk along a dirt trail and put a small treat in each of your footprints as you move forward. When your dog picks up the treats within these areas of your scent, he starts associating following food with following the track. Of course, there's more to it, but tracking nevertheless presents one of the easier sports for a novice trainer to learn independently through books and videos. Alternatively, a local training club may have someone who can put you "on the right track."

DISC DOG

If ever there was a breathtaking sport for dogs, disc-dog competition fits the bill. Spectators literally gasp as these trained dogs make astounding flying leaps and

Tracking gets an Aussie using his nose and his brain.

midair catches and somehow land on all four feet. Flying-disc competitions are sponsored by several organizations, with Skyhoundz being one of the largest; the goal is to earn regional, national, or world placements rather than titles. For most competitors, however, disc-dog offers an energy-burning and fun activity to enjoy with their dogs that requires less training than many other sports.

Safety always comes first, and owners interested in disc-sport training must keep in mind that a dog driving toward a flying disc may well run into something blocking his way while looking upward. Thus disc-play areas should be clear of obstacles and smooth underfoot, as a landing on rough, rocky soil can too easily result in injury.

Training a disc dog takes patience and time to build up to those gravity-defying jumps. It also helps if you can aim and throw a disc accurately. If you think that you and your dog have what it takes to get into serious disc play, ask your local training club if any of its members are active in disc dog, or you can attend competitions to see who trains in your area. In addition to competing, you may someday find you and your Aussie showing off for a crowd during halftime at one of your favorite football team's games.

CONFORMATION

In order to perform the variety of tasks for which the breed was originally intended, an Australian Shepherd needs proper

Before taking your conformation-quality Australian Shepherd to his first show, talk to your breeder, read, or watch a video about how to groom an Aussie for the ring. Far more involved than pet grooming, correct preparation of your dog for a show offers you a much better chance of winning the points.

conformation, or structure. Things that can be difficult for the average owner to detect, such as a straight shoulder or overangulated rear, can affect your dog's long-term working and athletic ability and lead to early arthritis, back issues, or other problems. Though no dog possesses a perfect structure, the closer your Aussie conforms to the breed standard—a description of the ideal representative of his breed set forth by experts from a national registering body—the more likely it is that he will be able to retain that "love-to-work" attitude even into his senior years.

Conformation shows, which most people know as "dog shows," are put on by breed or kennel clubs under the auspices of such organizations as the AKC and the United Kennel Club (UKC). Judges who are familiar with the given organization's official standard for the breed and who have been approved to judge the Australian Shepherd are brought in to evaluate structure and movement. Winning males and females earn points toward their championships by defeating a certain number of dogs in a show.

Beautiful as he no doubt looks to you, your Aussie may not possess the finer points, such as the correct eye shape, ear

set, or close-to-ideal structure that judges look for in the ring. For those who own show-quality dogs, participating in conformation offers an enjoyable and educational look into how all of the body parts should fit together and why. For the Aussie youngster, the show grounds bustling with dogs and people offer a wonderful socialization opportunity.

Keep in mind that what may look like an easy task of running a dog around the ring and standing him for the judge requires considerable training to do correctly. A poor handling job can make the best Aussie in the world look like he has a crooked back and a bull neck—and thus not a likely candidate for a prize. Contact a local training, breed, or kennel club or visit a dog show to learn more about handling.

HERDING/STOCKDOG

Not a casual pastime, herding or stockdog work requires regular access to livestock, preferably animals accustomed to being worked by dogs. Stockdog work is a dirty, all-weather type of activity that necessitates the guidance of an experienced trainer to prevent you, your dog, and the stock from getting hurt. Though trainers across the country offer this type of training, they may be a considerable distance from city or suburban dwellers. Despite the difficulties, many owners feel that the reward of putting their Aussies' instincts to work is worth the effort.

That said, not every owner or every Aussie takes to stock work, so before you rush out and buy a few sheep, attend a stockdog or herding competition to see the dogs in action. Contact your local breed or training club to find the nearest qualified trainer, who can help you determine if you and your dog have the potential for this

Playing disc with your dog is a great way to bond and give your dog a really good workout in just a few minutes at almost any time and in almost any place. Aussies have the high intelligence, drive, focus, energy, and endurance that make them fierce competitors in canine disc sports.

—Bob Evans, World Frisbee Dog Championship winner with
father/son Aussies from Georgetown, Texas

demanding work. If your dog tests well, you will experience the thrill of seeing your Aussie learn to understand his power to move stock as his herding instinct surfaces.

After awakening your dog's desire for the work, training focuses on teaching him how to move stock without unnecessarily scaring the animals while at the same time maintaining control and authority. The AKC offers herding tests and trials at different levels and with different types of stock, and the ASCA expressly promotes the working ability of the Australian Shepherd and offers titles to dogs in its herding trials on sheep, cattle, or ducks, with many dogs competing in all three categories. To further promote the breed as a working dog, the ASCA awards the Ranch Dog title to dogs that demonstrate to approved judges their ability to work cattle or sheep around the ranch or farm on a daily basis.

DRAFTING

While the Aussie's background revolved around working stock rather than carrying or pulling loads, most Aussies enjoy drafting activities surprisingly well—or perhaps this is not so surprising when you consider the difficulty that many owners encounter when trying to teach their leashed dogs not to pull.

Backpacking has become common for dogs both as a way to burn off more energy on shorter walks and as a way to allow the dogs to carry their own water or other supplies during longer hikes. You should always use a backpack made specifically for dogs to ensure even weight distribution and avoid chafing. Training starts with teaching your Aussie to wear the empty backpack; once he seems comfortable with that, put a lightweight item into each side. Gradually increase the weight until your dog is carrying a load appropriate for his size; it should never exceed 25 percent of his body weight and preferably should weigh less to ensure his comfort.

Pulling a cart (*carting*) or a skier (*skijoring*) requires considerably more training, as a runaway dog attached to a cart or a skier can hurt his owner, himself, and others in the process. Besides teaching your dog to wear a harness and how to pull, drafting activities require the dog to quickly respond to obedience commands. He must also resist the urge to chase a sudden temptation such as a darting bunny; this is particularly important for the skijoring dog pulling his owner along a snow-covered trail through woods teeming with wildlife.

Weight pulling is a less common sport that tests your dog's determination and strength as you encourage him to pull a minimum number of pounds loaded onto a sled, wheeled cart, or cart on rails. Because your Aussie couldn't outpull a Mastiff, dogs are divided into weight classes for competition, a system that allows breeds

Swimming is great exercise for a dog and is enjoyed by many dogs who are introduced to water properly.

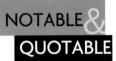

Competing...in dog sports is beneficial to both human and dog. The dog gets exercise and stimulation that make him easier to live with and be an enjoyable companion. The owner gets to get out, exercise, meet new people, develop friendships, and gain a loyal, well-trained canine companion in the process.

—Kirsten Cole-MacMurray, ASCA Versatility Award winner from Acton, California

All Aussies, working or companion, can test their instincts and skills in organized herding events.

from the smallest to the largest to enjoy this activity. Training begins with harness familiarization, then progresses to pulling light loads, and finally advances to competition weights.

Many different organizations sponsor the various drafting activities and sell supplies, so if a certain activity strikes your fancy, check the Internet or contact local training clubs to locate trainers and find upcoming events that you can attend as a spectator. You might finally give your Aussie a chance to pull to his heart's content.

THERAPY WORK

Taking your friendly Aussie to meet folks confined to nursing homes, hospitals, or other health-care facilities brings happiness and companionship to those who need a little cheer and perhaps miss their own beloved dogs. Even dog lovers are often surprised at the power of wagging tails and the happy offering of paws as people previously unresponsive to those around them suddenly form smiles and reach out to pet soft, furry ears. These instances prove common for those active in therapy work, sending owners walking away with smiles and sentimental tears.

If your dog can pass the Canine Good Citizen test and enjoys meeting people, chances are good that he will like doing therapy work. Obviously, your dog must become accustomed to wheelchairs, canes, walkers, and other medical equipment before entering a nursing home or hospital. Most facilities require visiting dogs to be certified by a recognized therapy organization, and such organizations offer appropriate training and testing to prepare dogs for therapy visits.

DOCK DIVING

Many Aussies love to swim and will happily dive into the water if given the chance. Dock-diving events offer your dog just that opportunity. Participants take flying leaps off the end of a 40-foot-long dock covered with suitable "launching" material. Dogs compete in different divisions called Big Air, Extreme Vertical, and Speed Retrieve, which translate to a long jump, a high jump, and a timed retrieve. To encourage the dogs to dive big, handlers throw favored toys or retrieving dummies for their dogs to chase into the water.

A favorite of dogs, handlers, and spectators, dock-diving competitions provide

The versatile and athletic Aussie will enjoy any activity that gets him out and moving—particularly with you!

entertainment for all. In some areas, finding a suitable and safe place to train can be a challenge, considering that the water must be deep enough for diving and free of underwater obstructions as well as be in a location that allows dogs. For those who find a suitable body of water, dock-diving training offers healthy exercise and a whole lot of fun. For more information, contact DockDogs, the sport's major ruling organization.

TRICKS

There are no titles, just fun, when you teach your dog to perform various tricks. Such training increases the bond between you and your Aussie, exercises your dog's brain, and entertains neighbors and guests. Many trainers use tricks as learning exercises for their dogs and to find out what

most motivates their dogs. Trick training proves especially useful for novice trainers who are learning the observation skills and timing necessary for proper use of the clicker before moving on to more serious competition training, such as for obedience or agility.

Tricks can range from jumping through hoops to packing a lunchbox to waving goodbye—the possibilities are endless when you combine a creative owner with a smart Australian Shepherd and fun, positive training methods. Some private trainers and a few training clubs offer classes in trick training, or you can buy a trick-training book. You don't need to be athletic, it doesn't require a lot of space, and Aussies love the attention, making it a perfect combination for owners who want to enjoy some lighthearted training.

S mart owners can find out more about the Aussie through the following organizations. Members will be glad to help you dig deeper into the world of Aussies—you won't even have to beg!

Academy of Veterinary Homeopathy: The AVH's membership of veterinarians and veterinary students is devoted to furthering education and research in veterinary homeopathy. The organization also certifies veterinary homeopaths. www.theavh.org

American Animal Hospital Association: The AAHA accredits small animal hospitals throughout the United States and Canada. www.healthypet.com

American Dog Owners Association: A nationwide group of dog owners and fanciers who promote responsible ownership and owners' rights. www.adoa.org

American Holistic Veterinary Medical Association: This professional organization for holistic veterinarians promotes alternative healthcare techniques and supports research in the field. www.ahvma.org

American Humane Association: This nonprofit organization founded in 1877 is dedicated to protecting children and animals. www.americanhumane.org

American Kennel Club: Founded in 1884, the AKC is America's oldest purebred dog registry. It governs conformation, companion, and performance events and promotes responsible dog ownership. www.akc.org

American Kennel Club Canine Health Foundation: This foundation is the largest nonprofit funder of exclusively canine research in the world. www.akcchf.org

American Society for the Prevention of Cruelty to Animals: The ASPCA was the first humane organization in North America. Its mission, as stated by Henry Bergh in 1866, is "to provide effective means for the prevention of cruelty to animals throughout the United States." www.aspca.org

American Veterinary Medical Association: This nonprofit association represents more than 80,000 veterinarians and is the accrediting body for American veterinary schools. www.avma.org

ASPCA Animal Poison Control Center: This resource, which is associated with the ASPCA, offers an informative website with lists of pet toxins and FAQs, as well as a hotline for animal poison-related emergencies that is available 24 hours a day, every day, at 888-426-4435. A consultation fee may be charged. www.aspca.org/apcc

Association of American Feed Control Officials: The AAFCO develops and implements uniform and equitable laws, regulations, standards, and enforcement policies for the manufacture, distribution and sale of animal feeds, resulting in safe and useful feeds. www.aafco.org

Association of Pet Dog Trainers: This international organization for professional dog trainers fosters continuing education among its members. www.apdt.com

Australian Shepherd Club of America: This national breed club, established in 1957, provides registration and hosts competitive events. Its website features breed education, breeder referrals, rescue information, and more. www.asca.org

Canadian Kennel Club: Our northern neighbor's oldest kennel club is similar to the AKC in the States. www.ckc.ca

Canine Freestyle Federation: The CFF is a volunteer organization devoted to promoting the sport of canine freestyle and holding demonstrations and competitions under its auspices. www.canine-freestyle.org

Canine Performance Events: An organization that fosters fun and competition through agility trials. www.k9cpe.com

Delta Society: This nonprofit trains and tests therapy-dog teams and aids in the implementation of animal-assisted therapy programs. www.deltasociety.org

DockDogs: This is the world's largest organization dedicated to competitive canine dock diving. www.dockdogs.com

Dog Scouts of America: Take your dog to camp. www.dogscouts.com

Fédération Cynologique Internationale: This international canine organization includes eighty-four member countries and partners that all issue their own pedigrees and train their own judges. www.fci.be

Love on a Leash: Share your dog's love with others. www.loveonaleash.org

National Association of Professional Pet Sitters: When you will be away for a while, hire someone to watch and entertain your dog. www.petsitters.org

North American Dog Agility Council: NADAC was founded in 1993 and holds competitive agility events through its sanctioned clubs. www.nadac.com

North American Flyball Association: NAFA was established in 1984 and is recognized as the world's governing body for the sport of flyball. www.flyball.org

Pet Care Services Association: A nonprofit trade association that includes nearly 3,000 American and international pet-care businesses. www.petcareservices.org

Pet Sitters International: This group's mission is to educate professional pet sitters and promote, support, and recognize excellence in pet sitting and to provide reliable pet sitters. www.petsit.com

Skyhoundz: This organization hosts the largest international competitive series of disc-dog events, sells disc-dog gear, and offers disc-dog training information. www.skyhoundz.com

Therapy Dogs International: This volunteer organization tests and certifies dog-and-owner therapy teams. www.tdi-dog.org

United Kennel Club: Established in 1898, this international purebred registry emphasizes performance events and education. www.ukcdogs.com

United States Australian Shepherd Association: The AKC parent club for the breed promotes ethical breeding, the formation of member clubs, competitive events, breed rescue, breed education, and more. www.australianshepherds.org

United States Dog Agility Association: This international organization founded in 1986 introduced the sport of agility to America; its Grand Prix tournament is one of the most prestigious competitions in the sport. www.usdaa.com

World Canine Freestyle Organization: This nonprofit promotes canine freestyle around the world for competition and entertainment. www.worldcaninefreestyle.org

CAR TRAVEL

If introduced to the car correctly, your Australian Shepherd will love going for rides. To ensure his safety and prevent him from creating distractions in the car while on the road, crate your puppy during his travels. Accustom your puppy to this by letting him spend some time in the crate when the car is not moving. Do this several times a day for a few days in a row and reward him with a few treats each time. You're teaching your puppy to view being crated in the car as something familiar and positive so he'll be fine with it when the car is in motion.

When you start taking him for rides, try not to feed him anything for roughly three hours prior, as food in his tummy increases

the chances that he'll throw up. Keep initial car rides short to help avoid motion sickness, as the more pleasant car travel is for him early on, the better. Drooling, panting, and an overall "I-feel-icky" look tell you that your puppy's probably about to get sick. Pulling over and getting him out of the car for a few minutes may settle his stomach enough for you to get home without incident.

Placing your puppy's crate behind the front seats rather than in the back of the vehicle may reduce the likelihood of carsickness. For unavoidable longer trips with a puppy prone to carsickness, ask your vet about a safe anti-nausea remedy that you can give him prior to traveling. Always take along extra bedding and clean-up items.

As your puppy adjusts to car rides and matures enough to behave nicely out of the crate, you can train him to wear a car harness that hooks to the vehicle's safety belt so he can look out the window.

PUPPY KINDERGARTEN

Puppy kindergarten classes help puppies with basic manners, obedience, and socialization skills. Most classes accept puppies at three to four months of age, after they've received the appropriate vaccinations. Classes vary as to individual lessons, but most puppy owners look for classes that teach puppies how to greet people politely, behave around other dogs, and walk without pulling on the leash rather than classes that focus mainly on obedience cues.

Observe a class in progress before signing up. A good puppy kindergarten instructor will show owners how to continue their puppies' training and socialization outside of class so that each person develops the skills that produce well-adjusted adult dogs. Most instructors allow puppy playtime to let the puppies have some fun while gaining doggy-language know-how, but an instructor should take care that no puppies get bullied or become bullies. Negative interactions could cause a puppy to develop fearfulness or aggression toward other dogs.

Puppy kindergarten generally lasts only seven to nine weeks, and training must continue far beyond this early introduction to manners and obedience. You can train on your own with videos, books, and magazines, but interpreting your Aussie's behavior and guiding him through adolescence usually is much easier with the help of experienced instructors. You might even find yourself among the star competitors in obedience, agility, or another sport who started out wanting a well-behaved companion but decided that training was too much fun to stop there.

HOME AND AWAY

Many people opt to take their dogs to doggy day care while they're at work. With a qualified staff dedicated to providing safe interaction and proper care, a doggy day care can be a godsend to a dog owner who is away from home for a period of time each day. You should carefully inspect a facility beforehand and talk to the staff about how they care for the dogs, what their experience includes, what services they provide, what they do when dogs don't get along with each other, and anything else that will give you peace of mind.

A well-run day care puts dogs together for playtime based on both personality and size, as even the friendliest Great Dane running with a Chihuahua can accidentally result in serious injury to the little dog. Also, if a dog takes a dislike to another dog, even if both get along fine with other playmates, they should not be put in a playgroup with each other. Day-care staff should be aware of such situations. Additionally, small playgroups of no more than ten dogs each are easier to handle and therefore safer than larger groups. Even with multiple people supervising a large group, one fight often prompts other fights, and damage can be done before all dogs are safely separated.

Other important safety and comfort amenities include blocked entrances to prevent dogs from escaping, dig-proof and jump-proof fencing around the outdoor areas, and naptime areas away from the group. Basically, the facility should provide a safe home away from home for your dog. Some doggy day cares offer webcam viewing to put worried owners' minds at ease.

BOARDING AND PET SITTERS

Though an increasing number of owners are taking their dogs along on vacations, this sometimes proves impossible. Many tourist attractions and lodging facilities don't allow our four-legged companions, even in outdoor areas, which means that you must find someone trustworthy to care for your Australian Shepherd while you're away. If you don't have a willing and able neighbor or friend to do it, you will have to either board your dog at a kennel or hire a professional pet sitter. It's important to inquire about the type of care and services provided and the experience of the kennel staff or sitter. If considering a boarding kennel, visit to inspect the overall facility and where your dog will stay. If you don't feel good about the place, look elsewhere.

Most dogs find staying in their own homes far more agreeable than being boarded. Some pet sitters will drop in several times a day to feed your dog and take him outside and then stay with him overnight, while others will settle your dog in his bed at night and return the following day. Work out details about your dog's care in advance, including instructions for any special foods and medications and making sure that the sitter has your veterinarian's contact information. The National Association of Professional Pet Sitters (NAPPS) certifies sitters who complete studies in pet care, behavior, business management, pet first aid, and more and can help owners find qualified local pet sitters.

IDENTIFICATION

Collars come off, leashes break, fences fail...these are just some of the many reasons that account for lost dogs. Supervision, training, and secure confinement rank as the top preventive measures, but despite it all, your Aussie could end up a sad statistic, especially without proper identification. Using multiple forms of ID—such as an ID tag, a collar with your contact information sewn into it, and a microchip—increase the odds of his return. If your Aussie loses his tag, he has the collar, and if he loses his collar, he has the microchip.

The microchip is a tiny device that contains a unique identification number that can be read with a scanner. The microchip number is then registered to you. Your veterinarian will inject the device between your dog's shoulder blades and test that it works by running a scanner over it to read the number. Many, but not all, shelters have scanners and routinely check incoming dogs for chips, but if your dog's chip cannot be scanned, it does no good. That explains why, even if your dog is permanently identified by a microchip, you must first do everything possible to prevent your dog from getting lost and then plan for the worst by ensuring that he wears ample identification. You should also keep current photos of your Aussie on hand in case you need to make lost-dog posters.

A dog riding loose in the car can equal the impact of a bowling ball if [he is] thrown against a window or person during an accident. For everyone's safety, your dog should always be secured in a sturdy crate or trained to wear a canine car harness attached to a seat belt when going for a ride.

—Mary Jo Stabinski-Heckman, owner of Paws 4 Thought in Eagleview, Pennsylvania

INDEX

AUSTRALIAN SHEPHERD, a Smart Owner's Guide®
part of the Kennel Club Books® Interactive Series®

LIBRARY OF CONGRESS CATALOGING-IN-PUBLICATION DATA

Cox-Evick, Christina.
 Australian shepherd / by Christina Cox-Evick.
   p. cm. -- (A smart owner's guide)
 Includes bibliographical references and index.
 ISBN 978-1-59378-783-7
 1. Australian shepherd dog. I. Title.
 SF429.A79C69 2011
 636.737--dc22

                    2010046405

JOIN
Club
Aussie™
TODAY!